RACING ON EMPTY

IONA ROSSELY

Sarah GRACE PUBLISHING

First published 2020 by Sarah Grace Publishing an
imprint of Malcolm Down Publishing
www.malcolmdown.co.uk

British Library Cataloguing in Publication Data
A catalogue record for this book is available from the British Library.

ISBN 978-1-912863-28-0

Cover design by Esther Kotecha
Photograph used by permission of Smirnoff
Art Direction Sarah Grace
Printed in the United Kingdom

DEDICATION

Racing on Empty is dedicated to my father, Bob McClure, who passed away a couple of weeks after I had finished writing the book. It was his drive, discipline, and pursuit of excellence that allowed me to have the education, willpower, and fortitude to never give up: no matter what life threw at me.

Love you, Daddy

WHAT OTHERS ARE SAYING...

I am so glad that Iona Rossely has written this book about how God has been at her side through her extraordinary life.

Nicky Gumbel

Racing on Empty combines just about everything I love in a memoir: top-level sporting achievements, a deep love of animals, a thoroughly relatable narrator, exotic international locations and authentic faith. Told with humour and honesty, Iona's book will help you make your own transition from racing on empty to running fulfilled. I highly recommend it.

Mark Stibbe, Bestselling and Award-winning Author

Iona Rossely has experienced life in a way many would dream of. She has skied professionally as a racer, she has professionally been involved in the elite world of formula one racing, and she has raced horses internationally. Yet in the midst of all of that she realised she was vitally missing something – a living relationship with Jesus!

As Iona began to know God and journey with Him she continued to live life, along with her husband, Jeff, passionately. Iona relates her journey with both candidness and humility. In the midst of Iona sharing vital experiences with God you never feel you're being preached at. Rather, you sense an invitation to jump into the deep end of your own set of adventures with God.

Reading *Racing on Empty* makes you feel as if you're sharing a roller-coaster ride with Iona, yet she conveys very powerfully the biblical truth that walking with God is going from strength to strength and glory to glory, even in the midst of the setbacks. Thanks, Iona, for sharing your very encouraging testimony!

Marc A. Dupont, Mantle of Praise Ministries, Inc.

If the saying 'What doesn't kill you makes you stronger' is true at all, then Iona Rossley is an extraordinary example of this truth. Iona's powerful life-story will not only move you, it will cause you to consider your own obstacles in a new way, and more than anything else, it will give you hope.

Cathy Madavan

Speaker, writer and author of Irrepressible – 12 principles for a courageous, resilient and fulfilling life

AUTHOR'S NOTE

To look back over one's life and remember every detail is a real challenge. I have relied on my memories, and thus the conversations, places and events evoke the feeling and meaning of what was said in all instances, so that the essence of the dialogue is more or less accurate. I have also changed some names but not all in order to maintain privacy.

ACKNOWLEDGEMENTS

Everybody I've ever met has had some input into *Racing on Empty*. Whether it was positive or negative, our journeys came together for a reason. So, it's a big thank you to you all.

My husband Jeff must get an award for patience. He reread my draft manuscripts over and over again. He could probably stand and recite the whole book, if asked. Thankfully, it was his memory, not mine, which managed to put events in the right timeline. I also have to acknowledge my stepmother Kathleen and my sisters Alison, Frances and Geraldine who, even though we rarely see each other, have supported me in everything I have done in the past – the good bits and the bad.

An enormous thank you to Bill Williams, whose consistent support and guidance opened doors into the world of publishing. My publisher Malcolm is more than a blessing. His professionalism and foresight have made this writing journey a reality. It was good to also work alongside someone who is just as competitive as I am.

Thank you Mark Stibbe, who mentored and inspired me to undertake two rewrites of *Racing on Empty*. Under his creative guidance, I saw the book transformed into one that told the story in a very real way. Mark's writing expertise literally put life into the words.

Lastly, there are no human words available to adequately thank God for his grace, patience and love. He never once abandoned me, even though I walked away from him so many times to pursue my own dreams. I'm blessed that I have the opportunity to record what happened.

THE SOZO FOUNDATION

All royalties from Racing on Empty will be given to the Sozo Foundation.

The Sozo Foundation is an NGO serving disadvantaged young people based in the township community of Vrygrond, Cape Town, South Africa.

Through interventions in education, skills development and social enterprise, the Sozo Foundation exists to support the 68 per cent of young people who are not in education, employment or training.

Life in post-apartheid South Africa sees Vrygrond desperately overcrowded and under resourced; one square kilometre home to 45,000 residents with, no high school, no police station and no clinic. Young people battle daily the dangers of crime, violence, addiction, abuse and gangsterism.

In the midst of these challenges stands the Sozo Centre, a facility and skilled team bringing hope by creating pathways to employment through education, skills and social enterprise. Many of these young people become the only breadwinners in the household and most of them first generation graduates in their families. Generational cycles of poverty, rejection and neglect are broken.

The golden strand which weaves itself though every member of the Sozo tribe is the unconditional love which they embody. It is the highest value in every training, tutoring and life skill session, transforming lives from the inside out, and against all odds rewriting the script for thousands of young people who encounter the truth that in this tribe 'you belong and you are loved'.

For more information on the work of The Sozo Foundation please visit www.thesozofoundation.org.za

CONTENTS

1
CONFINED

This was like a bad dream. It was my first night at the convent school in a dormitory with twenty-four other 11-year-olds. I lay there in a tiny prison-style bed with starched sheets, listening to a mixture of weeping and giggling echoing around the room. It was a night I would not forget. For the first time I understood the real meaning of being abandoned. I had never been separated from my mother or my three younger sisters before. Now I was stuck in a small town in the middle of the mountains in South Wales. A long way from home. I lay there staring into darkness with tears rolling down my cheeks. Everything felt dark and empty.

I vividly remember the time when my parents informed me that I was being sent to boarding school.

'Wow that sounds exciting. It's like something out of the movies,' I said.

I seriously got that wrong!

I remembered my mother's words as she left me at the school gates earlier that day. 'Don't worry Iona, you'll love it here. It will be character-building.'

'Yes, mummy and so is riding a horse,' I said, half-smiling.

Being painfully shy and not a social child, this felt like I'd been thrown into a lion's den. I tried not to look overly distressed, as I knew my mother was struggling emotionally. The whole family had been in turmoil for the preceding two months, since my parents announced they were to be divorced. I gave Mum a hug and held back the tears. *Could life get any worse?* I thought.

The days were packed with academic and religious activities. Neither of which I was passionate about. But I did enjoy playing in the lavish grounds and watching the squirrels leap from tree to tree. The main school building was an elegant old grey house comprising a maze of rooms that made up classrooms, study areas and an enormous library. Connected to the old house was a modern building that hosted the morning assemblies, all the gym activities and the evening recreation time. On the top floor were the bedrooms for the older students, while I slept in the old house in the large open dormitory. For those planning an escape into the town of Brecon it would mean scaling a twelve-foot brick wall – or you could just walk out of the front entrance, past the two lion statues and get picked up by a nun in less than a minute. And if you did manage not to get caught, then you might reconsider after a couple of nights out on the bleak mountain ranges of the Brecon Beacons National Park. Not advisable!

Even though I longed for the comforts of home, I remembered the cloud that hung over our disunited family. Everything had changed.

I recalled the day my mother found out that my father was having an affair. Her closest friend Annabella came over to console her. Watching my mother sob tore into my very being. I felt helpless. *How could my dad do this to my mum?* I wondered. Thinking that things couldn't get any worse, a week later it did!

We were leaving our local family church when one of my mum's friends gently pulled her aside and whispered in her ear. She went white and just seemed to freeze on the spot. We drove home in silence, not knowing what to say or do. *What had that lady said?*

'You're a bitch!' my mother screamed down the telephone. We all sat stunned, looking at each other. My mum never swore or used foul language. Never.

'You came here to comfort me and you're the one sleeping with Bob!' Her face was red, and tears streamed down her cheeks.

'Bitch!' She finished and then slammed the phone down. I could feel my bottom lip start to quiver as I struggled to hold back the tears. My dad and my mum's best friend!

We never talked about what happened. It was too painful. It was as if a darkness now hung over us. Our family was broken, and so was I.

Now at boarding school, I did not miss the daily pain of watching my mum come to terms with her new life. And I knew that having one less daughter to worry about would help. But I felt so empty and unloved. Now I was living in a bubble. I was totally isolated from the outside world, except for the one weekly phone call.

'Mummy it's too much. We seem to be in church all the time and most of it's in Latin. What's the point if you don't understand?' I cried down the phone. 'Besides if God was real, he wouldn't allow our family to split and he definitely wouldn't want me here.' I finished with my regular sign off, 'This is not normal. You need to come and get me now.'

She laughed every time and told me to hang on in there.

Even though my parents were both Catholic and regular churchgoers, I never once felt any longing to focus on anything religious and did my best to conjure up bailout plans on most of the religious activities. One of my favourite tricks in a church service was to position myself at the end of a pew and then take a nosedive into the aisle.

'Quick Sister Ursula, Iona has fainted again, poor child!'

I may have lacked self-confidence, but I had a rebellious streak. Academically I was horrendous; I just found it all very tedious.

Laughing, my new friend said, 'No one fails their 11-plus examination.'

'Well I have. Even better, I also failed the entrance exam for this school.' I was trying to be funny, but it just made me feel even more inadequate.

Unfortunately, Daddy had somehow persuaded the convent to take me in even though I had botched the exam. Money speaks louder than words!

My first year was bitterly hard, but things turned around when I realized that I was good at sport. This gave me the confidence I needed to overcome some of my insecurities. I was on the Welsh netball training squad, I represented the school in track races and I was the captain of the hockey team. But my passions were skiing and horse riding. From the age of two I had ridden. My bedroom told the full story. It was covered from floor to ceiling with winning rosettes for jumping, dressage, pony games and cross-country. Trophies adorned my bookshelves, with hundreds of photos of me and my ponies, none of which I ever owned. No matter how I asked or what I did, my father never gave in to my whining.

'Please, please, Daddy, this one's not expensive,' as I handed him a circled advert from the *Horse & Hound* magazine. So I begged and borrowed other friends' ponies; I normally got the ones no one else could ride or wanted to ride!

The highlight of my school weekend was being allowed out of confinement to gallop across the Brecon Beacons.

'Go Ginger, go!' I'd scream as I passed my classmates at breakneck speed, punching my fist into the air. My main goal was to ride the wildest and naughtiest horse available.

'Iona, slow down, you'll have an accident,' screeched our instructor. Sometimes I played deaf!

But the sport that gave me the most thrill was skiing. I was smitten. Every school holiday you would find me on the Pontypool artificial ski slope, located a twenty-minute walk from our house.

'Mummy this is important. I've been chosen to compete on the junior team, so you need to buy me my own skis and boots. It's much cheaper than a horse!' I continued, 'Skiing with hired equipment is not good for the image.'

My mum nearly always gave in to my demands. She became my rock when it came to ski competitions. She was always there to cheer me on and support me, rain or shine.

As the years progressed, I became a great deal more self-reliant, furiously competitive in all sports, and was beginning to bathe in self-glory in school and at home. I remember being slightly peeved when one of my classmates turned around and shouted, 'You think you're the bee's knees, well you're not!' She was probably right. I may have looked confident, but deep down I felt like a failure. Life just didn't make sense. I shone on the hockey field, the netball pitch and the ski slope – but emotionally I felt broken.

I walked slowly towards Mother Superior's office knowing I was in for yet another verbal scolding. 'Miss McClure, when you arrived here a couple of years ago you were a quiet, calm young lady. Where has she gone?'

'Is that a trick question?' I quietly asked.

She didn't smile.

My mother was called in on several occasions to discuss my behaviour and my possible removal from the school. My father only came when things got really serious.

'This is just one big playground for you, isn't it?' he said sternly. We had just left the Mother Superior's office after yet another warning.

The adult who influenced me the most in my early years was my father. With his Scottish military background and love of manners, our early childhood was run like a military camp. I loved him, even though he'd hurt my mum and broken up our family unit – and yes, I was scared of him. Like I was right now!

'Smoking, throwing toilet paper out of the window, cutting the heads off the garden flowers, escaping into town, meeting up with boys. Have I missed anything else out of your weekly adventures?'

It was best to stay silent.

'Do you know how much this school costs each term?'

Couldn't reply to that either, so remained in mute mode.

'You're throwing your life away. No education means no job. How are you going to survive?'

He did have a point.

This conversation also reminded me of one in my younger days. Daddy had sat the four of us on a couch in the living room and he paced up and down in front of us. 'I started out with nothing and I made a success of myself. You four need to understand that success and failure lands solely on your shoulders. I cannot do it for you. You have two arms, two legs and a brain. You can become whatever you want. I will pay for your education but after that, you're on your own.'

Tough and firm, that was my dad. Timely words and memories. It was exam year, so yes, I needed a reality check. I knuckled down and took my study a bit more seriously. It wasn't long before our GCE results were in. I had only completed eight exams, as I'd been thrown out of French and Maths in my second year. If you disrupt the class enough, they just ask you to leave. Easy! Unfortunately, it didn't work with all the nuns. I still hung onto the promise my dad had made. 'If you pass all your exams Iona, I will buy you a horse.'

'Miss McClure, Sister Vincent wants to see you again.'

What now?

She was smiling, which really worried me.

'This is a miracle! You passed seven and failed just one. So, there is hope.'

I was stunned into silence.

'That's the good news. The bad news is we have decided it's best you don't come back here for your A levels.'

I tried not to show any sign of joy.

Freedom was calling!

But without a horse.

2
FRESH TRACKS

So, what do you do after being trapped in a convent school for six years?

'Where is the vodka gone from the cabinet?' my mum screamed.

'What vodka?' I yelled from my bedroom, as I lay reading one of my skiing magazines. My mum did not miss a trick! 'You must have drunk it Mother dear.'

After that, I was frisked every afternoon as I left the house for my evening on the ski slope.

Life was good. I practically lived at the ski centre and just hung out with the lads. From 6 p.m. to 10 p.m. I was on the ski slope. And at the weekends, it was party time with my sisters. We all looked older than we were, and it was only on the odd occasion that we heard the dreaded, 'Can we see some ID please?' as we queued at the local nightclub.

Outside of partying and enjoying life, I started a one-year foundation course in art and design at Newport Art College. I was very much looking forward to this, but I must say, I look back now and can't remember anything positive about my experience. It didn't get any better when I was accepted into a degree course in fine art.

'I just feel so lonely at College, no one speaks to me. It's as if I'm an alien. Why am I the odd one out?' I told my dad as I sat in his office. He was now married to Annabella and seemed happy – but not with me. He sat staring at my pink hair and leather jacket. His expression wasn't one of approval.

'At least I had friends at the convent. Even the nuns liked me a little!'

I don't think he was listening.

To counteract my loneliness, I became even more obsessed with skiing. I took up weight training and jogging. I needed to be quicker, stronger and more agile.

'It's all about winning. Second and third place are not an option Iona,' my coach Colin screamed as I skied past him. 'If you want to be the best you have to work at it. There's no such thing as a free ride.'

Outside of my family, I had nothing else in my life but skiing. The hard work paid off when I savoured my first major successes in skiing. I won the Peter Stuyvesant Skier of the Year award two years in a row, and was invited to ski at the Daily Mail Ski Show in London. That was a seriously awesome experience.

As my passion for skiing increased, my love of painting diminished, and I knew I could not carry on at art college.

A door opened when a couple of friends decided to move to Switzerland to become ski instructors, one of which was my long-standing boyfriend David.

'Are you mad?' my father shouted.

'You've skied on snow once and now you want to walk out of your degree course, jump on a plane, to become a ski instructor. Please tell me this is a joke?'

Nothing was going to stop me. I had already made up my mind.

'You may think I'm irresponsible and thankless, but I'm not. I really need to do this.'

My mother was slightly less perturbed, but I still left feeling broken. I knew that this was the right move, but not having my parents' approval hurt deeply.

* * *

I stood at the top of a very steep ski run next to other apprentice instructors. The doubts started creeping in. *What have I done?* I thought. *I was 11 when I went on my first and last ski holiday. Maybe Daddy was right. I've gone mad!* My knees were shaking, my legs had turned to jelly, and I remember praying that if there was a God, now was the time to show up and help.

'If you fail this course, you're on the next plane home,' explained the head of the Ski School.

It's now or never! I thought.

My body bore the strain of the two-week course. My leg muscles hurt so much I was unable to walk down the stairs in our apartment. So, I sat on my bottom and bounced down instead. My flatmates thought it hilarious, but I didn't care.

'Mummy great news, I passed my instructor's exam. Can you believe that?' I shouted down the crackling phone line.

'Yes, I've been praying for you, Iona. That's amazing news!'

Even though I had to teach all the beginner groups, I was in paradise. I spent most of my free time working on improving my skiing, and the rest of the time was spent being one of the in-crowd. After a solid morning and afternoon of teaching, I'd stroll back to the chalet and rest my numb, frozen fingers on the radiator waiting for the pain to subside. I would peel off the many layers of clothing and then jump into a steaming hot bath and soak away the coldness.

With dinner out of the way, David and I and our mates would hit one of the many bars. I had no problem handling several 'Death Charges' a night: that's a beer with a vodka or apple liqueur shot. Rarely did I pay. My students would be climbing over each other to offer. But mostly it was one of the Swiss ski instructors flirting wildly in the hope that David was no longer on the scene.

One ski season rolled into another and all seemed rosy. My parents became a bit more understanding of my career decision, my skiing had improved immensely, and my love life seemed perfect. Having now moved in with David on a more permanent basis, I began to really feel that I finally had it all together. David and I had dated each other for about seven years. It was a fairly fiery relationship, with several breakups, but we always seemed to kiss and make up. However, this was all about to change.

'Will you take one of my skiing classes for me, darling?' David asked. 'I have another engagement.'

I never thought of asking what this other 'engagement' was, I simply said yes.

That afternoon I waited for David's class to show up. For some reason no one came, so I went off back to the village. On the way, I bumped into David's best friend.

'Have you seen David?' I asked.

He frowned. 'Let's go for a drink, Iona,' he suggested.

'Why can't you tell me now?'

'Let's go for a drink,' he repeated.

When we were sitting at the bar a few minutes later, he turned to me.

'I'm sorry to tell you this. David's cheating on you. He's in a hotel room with someone right now.'

My head was spinning.

'Who?' I cried.

'Some Page 3 model. I'm so sorry.'

It felt like I had been hit by a train. Holding back the tears, I stormed back to our apartment and collapsed in a heap on the bed, then I let go and the sobbing started. My heart was torn into tiny pieces.

A while later, David returned.

'You lied to me,' I said. 'I know who you were with. Get out. It's over!'

After he left, I phoned my mum. 'I'm coming home,' I cried.

I was miserable, angry and broken-hearted. I felt like I had fallen into a bottomless pit, with no way out. The pain of rejection seemed unbearable. For months, I disconnected from the world and turned inward. It seemed safer that way: no one could hurt me here. My mother sat with her arms around me. She rarely gave me a hug.

'Are you going to throw in the towel over one man?'

* * *

It took a change of scenery and a new adventure to catapult me back into reality. I was lined up to take my first British Ski Instructor's exam in Aviemore, Scotland. I decided that I didn't have the luxury of time to wallow in self-pity, so I focused on passing my exams, which would open more job opportunities for the next winter season.

As I verbally complained about the wind and the lack of visibility, the examiner smiled and said, 'Iona you've been spoilt. We don't all get the chance to ski in glamorous Switzerland. Skiing here will either make you or break you.'

I felt that I had been battered so much already I was more than able to rise to the challenge. I held back from making a cheeky retort. I was more concerned about how I was going to impress the examiners, skiing on iced rubble. This was going to be a first. I had heard stories about how difficult it is to ski in Scotland, but seriously, it was worse than I'd thought. To add to my concerns, David, my ex, was also in town. He had now risen up the ranks and was sought after in more ways than one. Being a tenacious soul, I focused on the job in hand. Even though it had been nine months since our break up – revenge did cross my mind.

The big day had arrived.

'McClure you made it. You passed with flying colours,' the head examiner looked over and handed me my Ski licence.

'Blimey, that's amazing!' I was overwhelmed.

'Iona you did it!' David patted me on the back.

I turned and looked at him.

Do I say what I really feel, or should I forgive? I wondered.

3
SCOTTISH MAGIC

I did forgive David, but it was hard. Really hard. I kept replaying over in my head what he had done. How could he have cheated on me like that, after seven years? But I really didn't want to drown in an emotional pool of bitterness, so I forgave him, on the condition that our relationship was purely platonic.

'It's a mind game Iona. If you harness your thoughts in a relaxed state, it will take you to the next level in your skiing.' David was eager to stay friends and help in any way he could. He handed me a box of cassettes and a book entitled *Sporting Body, Sporting Mind* and walked away.

I began to practise relaxation and visualization techniques, guided by the book and audio tapes. After several months my whole thought process had changed. I became more aware of everything. I was alert and calm and savoured every moment, it was almost as though time stood still. This heightened state of awareness gave me a new outlook. Not only did my skiing improve, but I also began to have this overwhelming feeling that there was a divine being looking over me. I remember having a real sense of a godly presence while accompanying my mother to church one Sunday. A rare occasion. It was so powerful that I struggled to hold back the tears. It was as if God was actually in the silence. I needed to understand what I was experiencing. *Why not ask a priest?* I thought.

As I drove to the church office, I was debating whether this was the right move, and at one point I nearly turned the car around. He sat behind his large mahogany desk with a stern look that would frighten most mortals, but I was on a mission and he may have the answer.

'While I do my visualization and relaxation, I feel a god-like presence in the room. Do you think that's God trying to connect with me?'

He smiled broadly, shuffled his portly body to a more comfortable position and with a deep, firm voice said, 'Young lady you're dealing with cult stuff, this is not what the church is about. Be warned. You're playing with fire!' He raised one eyebrow and looked at the door. It was time to leave.

No answers there! I drove away disheartened. I couldn't see how relaxing your muscles, monitoring your thoughts and visualizing your skiing could be deemed evil. I knew what I was experiencing. I knew there was something out there.

With winter approaching, I decided to take the bull by the horns and take up a real challenge. Instead of teaching in an exotic European ski resort, I opted for more of the iced rubble and gale-force winds. The coaching I would get within the Scottish Ski School would help me develop into a stronger, better all-round skier. It was a hard season. Some days the wind was so strong that you could open your ski jacket and go backwards up the hill on your skis. Scotland gave me an inner toughness, both physically and mentally.

But my favourite times in Scotland were not skiing or the nightly socializing at the Winking Owl pub, it was the time I spent on my own. My regular relaxation sessions were allowing me to become more aware of every second and every minute of my day. Some days I felt like I had been transported to heaven.

I recall the day I came across a pond surrounded by massive willow trees in a forest near my rented cottage. I sat on a rock and gazed into the pond. The world seemed to come to a grinding halt. But in this quietness, I became aware of a divine power lingering over me. It was overpowering and overwhelming. It gave me a feeling of utter peace and tranquillity. I didn't want to leave.

'Where do you go every afternoon?' Tracey asked.

'It's a secret.' I smiled.

'One day I will follow you,' she smirked. I knew she wouldn't, Tracey was always too busy trying to find the man of her dreams. Either on the slopes or in the Winking Owl pub.

* * *

The following season my career took a different turn. I was offered a ski instructor's job with an international tour operator, based in France at a resort called Les Arcs 1800. The resort was made up of three purpose-built ski stations, 1800, 1600 and 2000, that covered 2,000 metres of ski runs. It was a skier's paradise. The traffic-free resort had a mixture of modern stylish apartments and traditional chalets, surrounded by cafés and restaurants. This was glamour at its best. Skiing, teaching, drinking and eating delicious French food. I took my work and my skiing seriously. I taught six hours a day, but then at night, I morphed into the party girl. Frederick, one of the older instructors, was concerned.

'You need to make time to sleep. This is not a healthy lifestyle, Iona. One day you will crash and burn.'

I laughed and shot him a flirty smile. 'Life is short, so it's best to live it.'

But deep down I was searching inwardly and outwardly for something. I just didn't know what. *Was it love?* I mused. Maybe I should follow Tracey's example and go out hunting for true love. I tried not to delve too deep into my real feelings, just in case I unearthed something ugly.

'It's David on the phone,' came the yell from downstairs.

What does he want? I wondered.

'Iona, just felt I should call. How are the mind games?' He laughed as he asked the question.

'Non-existent, I'm afraid. Too busy. No time.'

'Don't waste the talent you have,' he said, and he hung up.

That didn't make me feel good! I had let myself slip into a fast-paced lifestyle that was not healthy. At the end of the six-month season I was exhausted, both mentally and physically. It was time to go home.

* * *

I loved our little white Welsh cottage. It sat perched on a hillside overlooking the caravan park we owned. The lush green lawns surrounded by beds of roses led into our secret forest where my sisters Alison, Frances, Geraldine and I would play hide and seek for hours on end. It was also a good place to sit and contemplate life. Which is where I sat now, contemplating.

I wandered back to the house.

'Mummy I'm so bored, I need to do something,' I whined.

'You sound like a teenager Iona.'

I sat down on the couch, which was covered with all my self-help books. Toby, my Old English sheepdog, came over and rested his giant head on my lap.

'Why not go up to the local reservoir and try sailing?' shouted my mum from the kitchen.

'That's for old people!' I laughed.

I sat on the grassy bank overlooking the reservoir. It was a hive of activity. Sailing boats ducked and dived as they negotiated the buoys, while the windsurfers tore full speed across the water, barely touching the surface. *Now that looks like my type of sport. Fast and challenging,* I thought.

I stood in the shop bewildered by the quantity of surfboards and sails. Suddenly a handsome dark-haired guy leapt over the shop counter.

'Your wish is my command,' he informed me.

Good sales pitch, I thought.

Three hours later, after sharing our life stories, I had my rig, a dinner date, plus several free windsurfing lessons. Not bad for an afternoon's shopping.

Carl and I became inseparable. He was an excellent teacher, and I was able to progress from beginner to an advanced windsurfer in less than four months. He also taught me how to water-ski.

'You're a natural Iona,' he yelled as he steered the boat, his dark curly hair bouncing in the wind. Our weekends were spent with his parents in their luxury caravan near the coast. We sailed, water-skied and ate seafood. Life was pretty cool.

'I've been thinking,' I smiled. 'I'm going to take my windsurfing instructor's exam so I can support myself in the summer months.'

Carl looked bemused and sad.

'You know you'll end up in some trendy beach resort. What about me? I can't leave my shop.'

I was chuffed he obviously thought I was going to pass. And flattered that he thought we had a steady relationship. I knew that many of my school friends had opted to prioritise their relationships over their career, but in the back of my mind I remembered my father's words: 'Never rely on anyone but yourself. You need to stand on your own. No matter what!'

This time I opted to follow my father's advice.

* * *

I couldn't stop giggling. With all the beautiful coastlines in the UK, I'd ended up in the city of Birmingham, surrounded by the aptly named Spaghetti Junction, one of the busiest highways in England. I stood next to the manmade lake in my wetsuit, listening to the constant hum of traffic and car horns.

Picking up on the mood of the group, our coach shouted in a high-pitched voice, 'You're not here for the view guys, so less of the sarcastic comments. You're here to learn how to teach windsurfing.'

I left the smog of Birmingham beaming from ear to ear. It might not have been the perfect location, but I was qualified. It also opened doors to a different type of challenge!

* * *

I sat looking over the table at a very handsome, tanned Jason. We hadn't seen each other for over six months. Jason had worked for the same tour operator as I had, as Chief Instructor, but in the ski resort next to mine. We had at one time been an item, but with a three-hour drive separating us, and hectic lifestyles, it was never going to work, so we opted to stay friends. We were in a quirky café overlooking Hayling Island Beach. Today was a catch-up day, or so I thought – Jason had something else in mind.

'Jason I've never competed in windsurfing. I've only just qualified as an instructor.'

'But it's an opportunity you can't miss,' he explained.

'Yes, to look like an idiot!'

My old ski buddy was not giving up. 'I can get you a sponsor. No problem.'

We weren't going anywhere fast with this conversation, so I took my takeaway coffee, gave him a peck on the cheek and excused myself. He did have a point – it was a one-off, high-profile event, but I was supposed to be working, not jetting off to Scotland to participate in an iron man competition.

One month later, I was in Scotland.

'You got me into this, so I hope for your sake I pull this off.'

'I thought you were competitive Iona?' Jason smirked.

The Salomon Gull Iron Man competition comprised a slalom race in the Cairngorms, followed by a windsurfing competition on Loch Morlich – snow to water. Branded from head to toe with the sponsor's logo, I gave Jason another 'you may regret this' look. But he was more interested in playing with his dog, who was also wearing a tailored waterproof jacket with the sponsor's logo on. It was just one big happy family!

One hundred and sixty participants stood huddled together waiting their turn to ski down the slalom course. It was on a fairly steep slope but, thankfully, I was one of the first to go, which meant fewer ruts. I knew my time was good, as it felt smooth and effortless. With my timed run over, I jumped into Jason's four-wheel drive. 'One down, one to go.'

The next day we stood looking at the calm flat lake.

'Where's the wind? It's always windy in Aviemore. Not today!'

'You'll have to create your own wind!' Jason said with a smirk.

My arms were heavy from pumping the sail, trying desperately to create my own breeze. This is not what windsurfing is about. It's called windsurfing for a reason. Suddenly a breeze came, and I was off.

'Go Iona, go!' I could hear the screaming in the distance. I crossed the finish line and collapsed on the shore, vowing never to listen to Jason ever again.

The loudspeaker echoed across the lake, 'It's time, it's time.' It took one hour to calculate the combined results of the ski and windsurfing races. I was packing my gear, just wanting to jump into a hot bath and go home. But Jason was adamant that I had placed in the top three. *Dream on Jason*, I thought.

'Iona, you won!'

'But how?'

'You just did what you always do. You did your best.' Jason was on cloud nine.

That was a surprise I was not expecting. And there were many more to come!

4
BAD MOVE

I sat on the beach, recovering from my two hours out in the surf. The sun felt good. It was a long time since I'd had a holiday. I watched Carl as he sailed off into the distance. I didn't have the stamina he had. I recalled our conversation a week earlier.

'Let's celebrate your win and go to Lanzarote,' Carl was so animated and happy. Rather shocked, I replied, 'I've only worked one month, I can't just leave my very first windsurfing job.'

'Listen, if Jason asked you, I bet there would be no hesitation.'

I laughed and strolled out of his shop. I think someone was jealous.

But I did go, and here I was on my first romantic holiday. Windsurfing, sunbathing, with good food and cocktails to finish the days. Heaven on earth. After ten days away, I was ready to go home. I needed to start my job applications for the forthcoming ski season.

I stood in the terminal watching the holidaymakers pile off the aircraft. I was travelling back on my own, as Carl had an important retail meeting with a potential customer. As I gazed across the runway, I spotted a familiar face. *That looks like Cindy*, I thought. *What is she doing here?*

I suddenly put two and two together. Carl wasn't meeting a client off the plane, it was his ex-girlfriend. 'The slimy toerag,' I said under my breath.

Stunned and numb I boarded the plane. *Is it me,* I thought, *do I have a sign on my forehead saying 'easy and stupid'?*

'I told you he was a bad egg, Iona.'

Jason meant well but it didn't help heal the scars. How many times can your heart be broken?

'I need to take a break from men!' I cried.

Broken, hurting and emotionally shredded, I dived back into my skiing career. Over the next couple of winter seasons, I continued working for the same tour operator and was eventually promoted to Chief Ski Instructor. This was a rare opportunity for a woman in this sport. It gave me the confidence to move forward with a bolder and more positive attitude.

In regard to my time out from relationships, I did start dating after several months, but I never allowed myself to get too involved. I built a wall around my feelings. No one could get in, and I couldn't get out!

* * *

I stood frozen to the spot, peering out through my iced-up ski googles. *Why do we do this?* I thought. I was back in Aviemore, Scotland to take my advanced instructor's exam. It had been three years since my last dose of the highlands.

'Sorry girls and boys, you'll have to walk up as the lifts are closed due to the wind.'

The only way to cope was to laugh. Unfortunately, I may have joked around slightly too much. Sam, our trainer, saw me imitating his style of skiing.

'McClure, since you seem to think you can ski better than me or anyone else in the group, let's see you ski the bumps.'

I threw myself into the challenge and, to Sam's delight, I crashed and burned. Big time! I think I may have lost a few brownie points trying to be a smartass, but the skiing conditions were beyond horrendous. How on earth could we be expected to demonstrate a ski manoeuvre when the trainer was unable to do it? The week did not go well for any of us, but I still lived in hope that I'd scrape through with a pass.

Failed. Failed. Failed. Failed. That's all I heard. Eighty per cent of the instructors were unsuccessful, including me. We all sat stunned. *Wow, that's a first!* I thought. I wasn't used to failing. I really wasn't sure how to process the results. This all seemed rather unfair. It was the worst pass-rate on record.

* * *

The following summer brought another first. I had applied for a job as a water sports manager on the beautiful island of Corfu, for a Christian organization, and to my surprise, I was offered the position. The directors were such a sweet couple, and seemed so loving and compassionate. They sat holding hands and never stopped smiling at each other or me.

'We will expect you to participate in all the Christian activities. This is all new to you, but it may take you on a journey that will change your whole perception on life.'

'Sounds interesting.' I was just so excited about finally getting a good summer job in a great location.

My first day set the course of things to come. Having offered to go and pick up some supplies from town, I managed to have my very first car accident. It was only a minor one, but I did scratch one of the locals' cars and lose a wing mirror off the company van.

As I walked into the boss's office, I was already preparing for the worst. 'I am so sorry, I'm just not used to driving on the wrong side of the road. I will pay for the damages.'

'Iona, my dear, these things happen. Don't fret!'

Malcolm and his staff were warm and kind. It felt like I had come into a ready-made family. 'But please take care we don't want you hurting yourself.'

Almost too nice, I thought.

My days were filled with teaching water skiing, windsurfing and hauling clients around on a large inflatable yellow hot dog.

'What's it like?' my sister Alison asked. I knew she was hoping for an invite out to the island.

'They sing lively songs, pray out loud and jump up and down clapping their hands in the worship services.'

Alison was intrigued. 'Is that normal?'

'Not sure, but they seem happy,' I explained.

'So, are you happy?'

I wasn't expecting that question.

'I hadn't really thought about it, but I do feel like I'm the odd one out.'

'Nothing new there, Iona.' And she hung up.

The modern whitewashed hotel stood high above the cliff edge, with a long, windy path that meandered down to the rocky coastline. There were no sandy beaches but the views from sea and land were stunning. I sat on the pontoon with my legs dangling in the cool water and watched yet another glorious sunrise. Sights like this made me think that there must be a God. Another sight I wasn't expecting that morning was a very large wild tortoise watching me from the corner of the wooden deck. It became a regular occurrence, until eventually he came and lay next to me. I named him Bradley and he became a bit of a tourist attraction with the guests. This place was beginning to feel like home, especially now I had a pet.

'Bradley, what are you doing?' I could see he was lying upside down with his legs in the air. 'Bradley get up, this is not funny,' I screamed as I ran towards him. But I was too late. This was now one very dead tortoise. I sat next to him and cried and cried. 'Don't leave me, please, Bradley.' *Why and how did this happen? Had someone poisoned my pet?* I wondered.

Days later, I'd worked out what had happened. Telling everyone that this tortoise was a pet sadly backfired. I had painted his name on his shell as a warning, a 'this tortoise is mine so hands off' type of gesture. Little did I know that the household paint would filter through into his bloodstream and poison him. Life went on, but without Bradley.

All of our weekly guests arrived happy and left even happier. *Am I missing something?* I mused. *I don't feel what they feel.* Feeling confined and a little claustrophobic, I decided to explore town.

'Angela, are you up for a night on the town?' Angela was the only one who, like me, was a little on the wild side.

'Thought you'd never ask. Let's do it!' She cried with excitement. And we did. Over and over again. Every night, without fail, we were in Angela's words 'painting the town red!'

'Iona are you sure this is a good move?' Angela asked one day. I knew she was concerned.

'Carlos is charming, handsome and kind. There is no such thing as the perfect man. We all know that!' I laughed.

'But why resign your job and move in with him? That's extreme. You've only been dating him for three months!'

'I'm going to assist in running his water sports school. Same job, just different employer. Angela, we can still meet up for drinks in the evening, if that's what concerns you.'

'It's not that. It just doesn't feel right,' Angela said, looking sad.

I had met Carlos on the very first night that Angela and I had ventured out. He strolled into the wine bar as if he owned the place. Everybody greeted him and either shook his hand or patted him on the back. Angela watched.

'Must be one of the local dignitaries.'

'Yep, I wonder who he is?'

As the night rolled, on Carlos made his way slowly over to our end of the bar.

'Ladies, you must be new in town,' he said while winking at the barmaid.

Angela jumped in, 'Nope not new. We just keep a low profile!'

Night after night we met Carlos at our end of the bar. We laughed and chatted and exchanged stories. Carlos owned one of biggest water sports schools on the island, so we had plenty to talk about. When he invited me out for dinner, I knew deep down this was a bad move. But I still did it!

Within a couple of months of working for him, I knew things weren't right.

'Carlos, why do you react every time I speak to a man? I am not a china doll and you don't own me,' I screamed at the top of my voice. The music was so loud in his living room my ears were hurting.

'It's probably best you stay in at night Iona.' Carlos was being serious. This was like something out of a horror movie. I knew it was time to leave, but what if he turned nasty?

'Angela he's gone out for a couple of hours, I'm leaving now.' With suitcase in tow, I jumped on the bus that would drop me back at the Christian hotel, just outside the village. Angela was at the door waiting. My heart was pounding, and my legs were like jelly. I was scared and worried about how Carlos would react when he returned to an empty house.

'What if he comes looking for me?'

Angela gave me a big hug. 'You're safe here Iona.'

Twenty-four hours later, I was on a luxury coach with a bunch of jolly Christians on the way to the airport. *Never again do I want to experience anything like that*, I thought as I stared out of the coach window.

I was angry with myself. I really didn't like what I was becoming. Why did I leave such a good job for a man old enough to be my dad? And these Christians just welcomed me back with open arms, and even organized my trip home. Tears rolled down my cheeks. Why do I make my life so difficult?

5
THE FLYING KILOMETRE

If there's no one around to give you a kick up the posterior, then you have to do it yourself. So, I did! I refocused and set about sorting my life out. I was now back as Chief Instructor in Les Arcs, but at the higher ski station, Les Arcs 2000, which was well known for its speed skiing track called the Kilomètre Lancé or in English, the Flying Kilometre. I would watch in amazement as these speed skiers hurtled down the track at speeds of more than 160 km/h. It did look impressive, but I couldn't see the point of travelling in a straight line, it seemed rather meaningless.

'We should all have a go on our day off,' Belinda said while bouncing up and down on the couch like a schoolgirl. I was hosting our weekly instructors' meeting.

'Yes,' agreed Arnold. 'You cannot work here and not try speed skiing!'

The remainder of the group, all ten of them, nodded and did their customary high fives. I cannot say I was leaping around with excitement but I agreed to join them.

As we were all new to speed skiing, we were only allowed to start from below the halfway point, so we didn't pick up too much speed. To be honest, I really wasn't looking forward to this, but my pride wouldn't allow me to chicken out. Friday came around, and after collecting my hired helmet and 2-metre-long skis, I took the lift to the designated meeting point. I nervously made my way to the track but was surprised not to see any of my skiing colleagues.

I arrived at the starting point to find one marshal with his walkie-talkie, but no one else. Where are the others? Had I got the time wrong? I suddenly had this awful feeling that I'd been set up!

The sturdy looking marshal looked at me and asked, 'Are you okay? You look a bit scared.'

'Yes, I'm terrified.' No harm in being truthful.

There was no backing down. I had no choice. The only way down was on the track, unless I totally wimped out and walked down. I knew my charming, caring friends were all at the bottom having a laugh. I looked down the track. It was steep. Really steep. I could see the finish line and the outline of the second marshal who looked like a tiny ant in the distance. *That's a very long way without turning*, I thought. My legs were shaking, my heart was pounding. I felt like a lump of jelly. Probably looked like one as well.

'Now before you start, let me show you the best position. So, you can get up a good speed,' said the very excited marshal.

'Yes, that sounds like a plan.' I was being sarcastic, but the marshal ignored it and proceeded to demonstrate what he called the 'egg' position. I momentarily laughed, as I had an image of me as scrambled egg plastered all over the track.

'One question, what happens if I fall?' I said in jest.

'Probably best not to!' he said.

Okay that was reassuring!

I sheepishly manoeuvred my skis into the starting position and took a deep breath. It felt as if I was going to jump out of a block of flats! I pushed off gently. Within a couple of seconds, I felt like I was flying. This was the fastest I'd ever been on a pair of skis. It was exhilarating and scary. The same sensation as you get on a rollercoaster when you suddenly drop off the lip into a downward dive and leave your stomach behind. My heart was thudding in my ears, and my legs were still jellified as I hit the upward dip that slows you down.

Wow, that was a rush! I thought.

'Good one Iona, good one!' my crew shouted, clapping and cheering. 'Way to go!' They screamed.

I was unable to speak. The adrenaline was still pumping through my body. I needed to get my breathing under control, so I could talk without slurring.

I balanced myself on my ski sticks and grinned.

'Okay, who's next?'

Silence. No one spoke.

'Fine. I'm going up for a second run.'

To my amazement, my first recorded run was 86 km/h and the second was even faster, 96 km/h. I was still scared to death and shaking prior to my second descent, but when I was actually on the track, I loved the exhilaration and the feeling of speed.

Later, as I gazed at my bedroom ceiling waiting for sleep to come, it felt as though a fire had been ignited deep within me. I kept replaying my two runs down the Flying Kilometre over and over in my mind. For the first time in a long time, I felt like I had really achieved something. I had pushed through my comfort zone and had come out the other end. And it felt good. Really good.

'I hear you're a bit of a speed merchant young lady,' shouted Michael as he was making his way up the pommel lift. Michael was head of the French ski school and was also a very charming friend, who was a great support. As I was not fluent in French, Michael had got me out of some sticky situations.

'Iona, come and speak with me when you have time.'

'Will do,' I shouted to him as he disappeared into the distance.

The next day, still buzzing from my speed skiing experience, I waltzed into Michael's office. He gave me the customary three kisses and patted me on the back.

'Your speeds were good yesterday. Really good for a first timer.'

'Thank you. Can't wait to try again!'

'We can help you if you're interested in racing. There are not many lady skiers, so we can waiver the track fee and the hiring of the helmet and skis. At least then you can get on the slope and practise.'

'Wow! Thank you. I wasn't expecting that.' I gave him a big hug and left practically skipping out of his building.

Knowing I had a long way to go before I could ever seriously compete, I researched as much as I could on speed skiing, the races, the competitions and the training. When the Flying Kilometre was opened for the professionals, I would plant myself next to the track. I watched them as they shot passed like a speeding bullet. The noise they made was like the rumbling of thunder. I knew this sport was not for the timid but for the risk-taker. The speed skier had two objectives: to obtain the fastest possible speed in a particular race or establish a new world record. With the top skiers reaching over 200 km/h, and talks about it being a potential Olympic sport, speed skiing was now seriously on the map.

To even have a chance of playing with the big guys I needed to get into shape, so that I could handle the forces of high-speed skiing. I was fairly fit, but I knew I needed to work on my resistance training and build more muscle. But beyond the physical requirements, the one thing I kept reading and hearing about was that the skier's mental attributes were just as important. It looked like my relaxation and visualization training needed to be reintroduced into my daily routine.

'Not seeing you out at night so much. Is this old age creeping in?' said Frederick, the restaurant owner.

'Very funny! I'm taking life a bit more seriously and I'm working out physically and mentally,' I said as I gazed at the menu, already knowing what I was going to order.

'Same as usual please, Frederick.'

Shortly afterwards, a sizzling plate of frogs' legs in garlic butter appeared with a bowl of steaming French fries.

'This will help you build muscles!' he said, as he placed my dinner in front of me.

Practising on the Flying Kilometre track came with its own frustrations. Mainly in the form of not knowing when the slope would be open. For safety reasons, the track needed to be groomed regularly, plus marshals needed to be in place and the timing equipment monitored. If we had a snowfall, then I knew it could be a week or two before the slope would reopen for practice runs.

I was running in the mornings, weight training late afternoons and doing my visualization techniques in the evenings.

'Did you know your mind doesn't know the difference between imagination and reality?' I told Belinda. 'I visualize myself racing down the speed track at 200 km/h while lying in my bedroom.'

She laughed and said, 'Then why bother with the real thing, when you can stay indoors. It's probably safer!'

'Very funny Belinda!'

I knew my thoughts had a great deal to do with how I would perform in a race situation, so I spent hours on my mental exercises. Feeling stronger and fitter, and mentally calmer, my practice speeds carried on improving. It was time for my first competition.

6

STAR WARS AND VODKA

With speed skiing seen as a risky and sometimes dangerous sport there were only a handful of speed skiing tracks in Europe, which meant only a couple of races per season. Thus, I just went for the one and only race left for the season: the 1986 World Championships.

Armed with my hired skis and helmet, I arrived at the French Ski resort of La Clusaz. This quirky boutique-style resort with its wooden chalets and horse-drawn sledges was one of the prettiest places I'd ever seen. Thankfully, the tour operator I worked for also had a ski school in the village, so they kindly allowed me to stay in their hotel for the week.

I sat outside on the bar terrace overlooking the main street.

'Busy. Busy. We have been bombarded by speed skiers from all over the world.'

I turned around to see a large burly man with his hands on his hips smiling down at me.

'Same reason I'm here!'

He looked surprised. 'You don't look like one of them.'

I wasn't sure what he meant by that, but I choose to take it as some kind of compliment. *Maybe they were all big and ugly*, I thought.

I had officially registered as a competitor a month earlier, so I was aware of the practice times and the schedule building up to the one-day race. After signing in at the organizers' office, I went to check out the speed track.

'You must be Iona McClure.'

Standing in front of me were the two brothers Graham and Stuart Wilkie. I recognized them from the speed skiing magazine photos. They were both talented and successful speedsters and had jointly put speed skiing on the UK map.

'Nice to have another British lady representing our fair island,' said Stuart.

'Pleased to meet you. Feel like I already know you both.'

We chatted for a good hour, and they kindly offered to help in any way they could.

The race had attracted just under two hundred skiers from across the globe. These were the fastest men and women on skis, all of whom were now standing at the top of the run looking down. Two days of practice was allocated so skiers could get a feel for the slope. I stood waiting for my turn to go. It didn't look as steep as the track at Les Arcs, but it was still an extreme incline. Even in the practice sessions, there was silence at the start. I got to meet many of the other skiers as we side-stepped up the side to the top. I introduced myself to Davina Galitza, the British Ladies Champion. Slightly overwhelmed by being surrounded by several past World Champions, I breathed a sigh of relief when I met another couple of amateurs who were newbies like me.

This was a sport where men and women competed on equal terms. Same track, same equipment. They did, however, divide racers into professional and amateur sections.

Due to the risks involved with skiing at high speeds, the races were carefully structured so that only those skiers with the best-timed runs could proceed to the next level. Thus, each race would start at a lower point on the track, and if their times were good enough, contestants were able to move higher up the track to start. This normally guaranteed that only the better skiers had the chance to gain the higher speeds, as the slower ones got knocked out.

Race day arrived. Standing at the top, waiting for my name to be called was a nerve-wracking experience, but I still managed to laugh at my surroundings. It looked like a movie set of *Star Wars*. Everywhere were Darth Vader look-alikes wearing aerodynamic helmets and brightly coloured Lycra suits: it felt rather surreal. These racers came in all shapes and sizes, all immensely strong and fit. I remembered the man's comment a couple of days ago, saying I didn't look like a speed skier. I was probably the shortest in height and frame, but nothing else stood out. I was wearing a custom-made luminous pink skin-tight Lycra suit, with a small set of fairings (little wings) attached to my calves to reduce wind resistance. I felt like I fitted in with the crowd.

'Remember your first run is important. You need to finish close to the time of the fastest skier. Slower skiers don't get a second chance,' said Stuart as he wished me luck.

My first run felt smooth and in control. I stood at the bottom, not knowing whether I had made it to the second round.

'McClure you're through!' bellowed the loudspeaker.

We had now climbed way up into a gully, and the hundreds of spectators looked like grains of sand. The adrenaline was pumping through my body. I stayed focused on my breathing and waited for my number to be called.

'Number fourteen.'

I shuffled my 240-cm skis around and pointed them down the track, while bearing weight on my poles. I had spent several months getting ready for this moment. *It's now or never*, I thought. And I pushed off.

I felt like I'd jumped out of a plane. Even though the wind was buffeting my body I felt strong in my position. *Next best thing to flying!* I thought, as I hurtled down the track. In a blink of an eye, I had passed the laser that records your speed. *Wow! That felt fast. But was it?* I slowly stood up and raised my arms, while moving my skis into a snowplough. My heart was still pounding, my body felt alive with adrenaline. That felt good!

But how fast did I go? I wondered.

I waited and waited. I strained to hear over the clapping and cheering. 'McClure speed off 159.9 km/h.'

Wow! That was the fastest I'd ever skied. I was absolutely elated.

The rest of the day was a bit of a blur. I was so excited, I could hardly focus on anything except replaying my last run over and over in my head. But I did stay and watch the professionals as they sped past at incredible speeds, reaching 200 km/h and more. They were in a totally different league. Something to aim for!

The party atmosphere on the slopes eventually moved into the bars. I felt at home with my new friends, as we relived the thrills and spills of the day, and discussed the next races on the world calendar.

'I cannot afford to race all over the world,' I said.

Sasha, one of the other speed skiers, leant across the table with yet another drink for me. 'Iona, go get some sponsors. If you don't ask, you won't get. It's that simple.'

Just as I was working up a reply, Stuart and Graham Wilkie came over to the table. 'Here you go Iona,' said Stuart as he handed me a piece of paper.

'Congrats, you are now the 1986 Ladies British Overseas Champion.'

Shocked and overwhelmed, I looked at the Wilkie brothers, leapt to my feet and gave them both a big bear hug.

I left La Clusaz feeling exhilarated and full of confidence. But I knew that in order to move up a level I would need to get financial backing. My instructor's salary was good, but it wasn't enough to allow me to take time off every couple of months.

I knew I had to put an action plan together in order to gain sponsorship, so when I returned home to Wales a couple of months later, I started the ball rolling by ringing all the local newspapers. I was convinced that if I could get some press coverage, I could find a sponsor. I called several newspaper editors.

'Yes, hello, my name is Iona McClure and I'm planning to be the fastest lady on skis in the world. Would you like to interview me?'

Most of them had never heard of the sport. So, having some young woman ring up out of the blue who thought she could be the next world's fastest speed skier may have led them to think I was slightly insane or just a local oddball. Not surprisingly, they all hung up, except one lovely gentleman, who was intrigued. I only needed one and I knew the others would follow. Over the following two months, I had gained enough press coverage to approach potential sponsors.

'I need to borrow your car Mummy. I have an interview in Blackpool,' I shouted from my makeshift office in the lounge.

'Yes, on the condition you don't get any more speeding fines.'

Smirnoff Vodka were already sponsoring a very talented Scottish speed skier called John Clarke. As they were heavily involved in the sport, I hoped that maybe an up and coming lady skier would be perfect for them.

Their public relations company, Cartmell PR was run by Gary Cartmell. As soon as I walked into his luxurious office I knew I would have to be 'beyond confident' in my sporting goals. Gary was direct and to the point.

'Great Iona, but let me think about this. I will call in a couple of days.'

We shook hands and I left.

Deep down I believed I had done enough to win him over, but as the days drifted by without a call, I began to wonder.

'Iona you cannot sit on top of that phone. You do have a life outside of finding a sponsor. Why not take Toby for walk?'

One week of waiting and nothing.

'There's a call for you. Some man from the north,' called my mum as I was outside giving Toby his daily groom.

Covered in white fur, I launched toward the phone. I listened intently, replied, 'No problem,' and put the phone down.

My mother, realizing it was Gary, was glaring at me. 'Well, yes or no?'

I collapsed onto the couch, stunned. 'He said yes. We're meeting next week to sign contracts.'

Very rarely have I seen my mum perform an Irish jig, but this was one of those occasions.

The realization suddenly hit home. *Now I'm seriously going to have to up my game!* I thought. Thankfully, I had the whole summer ahead of me. David stepped in to help draw up a fitness programme that would allow me to be in peak condition for the start of the racing season. My days were filled weight training, running, sports meditation and skiing. Fortunately, I had time to work on myself both mentally and physically.

Or did I?

7
STITCHED UP

'New Zealand, are you serious?'

I was perched on my office desk underneath our open-style staircase trying to take in the news from this phone conversation.

'We'd like to invite you to race in New Zealand at the 1986 FIS World Series in September. It's a really good opportunity. One you shouldn't miss,' announced British speed skier Stuart Wilkie.

'That would be awesome. But I'll need to get Smirnoff's approval.'

I put the phone down and sat stunned. I was blown away. How exciting. Thoughts started bombarding my mind: *Would I be ready for this? Would Smirnoff agree to financing the trip?* First I needed to speak with Smirnoff's PR Agency. It all hung on them.

With only a couple of months to departure day, I was still waiting for Smirnoff to decide. Every day seemed like a month. But this was not my only dilemma. My mother now had a few things to say about the possible trip.

'You're not going without me and that's non-negotiable!' my mum warned. I was horrified. She had to be kidding! *My first international race as a professional and my mum wants to come. I will be a laughing stock*, I thought.

'I am deadly serious. You cannot travel across the other side of the world on your own.'

'I won't be on my own, I'll be with several guys.'

My mother looked at me and pointed a finger, 'Exactly! I rest my case.'

I thought it best not to discuss this further. I believed that if I just left it, after a week or so she would change her mind and see sense.

One week later, I had my answer from Smirnoff. 'We have a green light,' I screamed with excitement.

'That's brilliant. I'll book our flights,' shouted mum.

We finally came to an agreement. She could come, but on the condition that she pretended to be my sister. My mother looked about 15 years younger than she was, maybe more, so I was sure we'd pull it off.

London to Auckland was a long flight but the stopovers in Singapore and Australia made it bearable. After an interview session with the Auckland media, we trundled off to the Turoa Ski Station and settled in before a day of practising on the Mangaehuehu Glacier. But things did not go to plan.

I stood at the top of the course ready to take my first practice run. I did a quick check of my bindings to confirm they were on the right settings, readjusted my helmet and pushed off. Halfway down the track, I suddenly felt extremely dizzy. The next thing I knew, I was hurtling out of control with arms and legs swirling around as I bounced and slid down the course. When I finally came to a stop, I lay there winded and shocked, wondering what on earth had happened.

I was sledged off the mountain to the hospital to find out that my right leg now had a small hairline fracture. Not what I wanted to hear!

After a complete medical check, they also found the cause of my fall. 'Simple. You have an inner-ear infection. Your balance would have been seriously affected at the speed you were travelling,' said the charming doctor. 'It's very common on long flights. But the good news is it's easily treated. The bad news is that I cannot give you medical clearance for you to race if the ear infection is not totally gone.'

I could not believe what I was hearing!

'Doctor, I have flown from the other side of the world for this race. Plus, my sponsor will have a meltdown if I don't race.'

I looked at him with a desperate 'there must be something you can do' look.

'I have three days,' I pleaded.

'Okay, but I'm not promising. It normally takes five days to clear an ear infection.'

I was scheduled to come back the day before the race. I had no idea if I would get a medical certificate. The hairline fracture was seen as a minor injury, as it was above my boot line. So that was one consolation.

'You need to tell Smirnoff that you might not be racing.'

'Mother that's not sensible! They will freak. Let's wait and see.'

And that's what we did. While the other skiers all had three days to practise, I sat and watched. It all seemed very unfair. *Why me?* I thought. And if I did get clearance to race, without any practice runs on the course, would I be ready?

'You're good to go Iona. The gods are smiling on you,' said the doctor as he handed me the medical clearance. I gave him a big bear hug and skipped out of his surgery.

It's strange that when things start badly, there is sometimes a silver lining that propels you into a different mindset. It was time to get stuck in and pull a rabbit out of my hat. I refused to acknowledge the negative thoughts; instead I replayed my visualization techniques and was ready to go.

I stood at the same spot and looked into the distance. It was a beautiful day. I felt strong and positive. *You can do this Iona.*

I had two runs both of which were smooth and incident-free. On the second attempt, I recorded a speed of 134 km/h. Not fast, but the track was slow. It was enough to win the ladies' section and walk away with the title of 1986 New Zealand Ladies Champion.

That night we celebrated. Maybe a bit too much. I had decided to put pink streaks in my hair, with a couple of feathers and arrive as a Red Indian.

'I didn't realize it was fancy dress?' Stuart said laughing.

'Nothing wrong being bright and colourful,' I smiled.

The champagne and the beer flowed freely that night. So much so that I let slip our secret!

'Mummy, don't drink too much.'

Suddenly the room full of more than eighty skiers went silent. And my mum ducked under the table.

Oops, I think I've let the cat out of the bag!

'So, Josephine is not your sister?' said Henry, one of the New Zealand skiers. The room just erupted into laughter.

A couple of days later, after resting up, we were ready for yet another adventure. The organizers had hired a guide, so that we could go helicopter skiing. With my hair still pink, but minus the feathers, we all clambered into the helicopter. The two Wilkie brothers, Henry, James, me and our guide peered out of the windows as we soared over the snowy mountain range of Coronet Peak. This was a totally different experience for me.

Thankfully, we had a professional ski guide to follow, which in itself is great, but not when you have several international speed skiers who are not used to travelling in an orderly manner. Our tall lanky guide seemed aware that we were all speed merchants, so we were given a little pep talk prior to departure.

'Remember, do not overtake me. I know the mountain. There are many cliffs and crevasses. So please ski carefully and stay behind me.'

I had no intention of overtaking him, so I was happy to stay behind. Off we went, all eagerly jostling for position behind the guide. Our guide, unaware of how close we were all packed in behind him, suddenly stopped.

Even though it all happened so quickly, everything seemed to go into slow motion. As the guide stopped, so did Henry, who did a quick sideward stop across the top of my skis. This meant I was unable to turn, so I kept going and went head first into Henry's ski pole, then flipped over the guide and fell down into the hollow he was trying to avoid.

All I felt as I went flying through the air was a cold sensation and pain near my nose. Henry's ski pole had actually gone into the side of my nose and up into my sinuses. There was blood everywhere. I cannot remember much: it was as though my body had shut down because of the pain. I couldn't feel a thing. I just felt numb all over.

I was helicoptered off the slope to Dunedin Hospital. As I was rushed into emergency, I couldn't figure out why so many people were looking at me strangely. The medics had wrapped my whole face in bandages and had left one hole for me to peer out of. But with the flowing pink hair sprouting out of the top of the bandages, no one was quite sure what was underneath.

I lay in my bed in a private room gazing out of the window. My head hurt. My face hurt. Now I was the proud owner of ten stiches and two black eyes.

The doctor sat on the corner of my bed.

'You are one very lucky lady. It could have been a great deal worse.' He stood up and did a quick check of my stiches. 'The surgery went well. We hope you won't need a skin graft. But you're going to have a great scar.'

I tried to smile but it hurt.

'How long do I have to stay here, doctor?'

'Probably a week. But you won't be flying home just yet. The ski pole broke through your nose and sinus, so the pressure would be too much at altitude.'

Why am I so unlucky? I thought. The accident was no one's fault. It was just a freaky mishap. Staring up at the white ceiling, I was full of mixed emotions. I felt good that I'd made a comeback after my fall, but was feeling down in regard to two hospital visits in less than ten days. Time passed slowly. The only visitors I had were the nurses, as my mother had left after the ski race to stay with friends on the South Island, and it was a while before we managed to contact her.

My mother stormed through the door with a very worried expression. 'I told you that you needed a chaperone. I leave for one week and you're back in hospital.'

I thought that was a strange thing to say, as she'd been with me when I'd ended up in hospital the previous week. But thought it best not to mention it.

She stood with arms on hips looking at me. 'And look at your face. What a mess!'

The next major hurdle was getting back to the UK. I was due to compete at the Westland Helicopter Base in the UK in the Smirnoff Aerodynamic Challenge in less than ten days. Smirnoff had invited the top speed skiers from across the globe to compete in a wind tunnel race. I had no idea what a wind tunnel race was but was up for the challenge.

'If you were my daughter, I wouldn't let you fly. However, considering what you've been through you can leave, but take the medication and nose drops,' the consultant advised.

'You're the man, doctor! Thanks.'

As we flew over the beautiful New Zealand coastline, I couldn't help but chuckle to myself. I was leaving with a hairline fracture, broken sinus and nose plus a scarred face and two black eyes. I felt that I'd had my share of bad luck. Or was this just the start? I was also thinking that I should have told Smirnoff about my helicopter accident. But I didn't. Bit late now!

8

FOUR WHEELS ON MY WAGON

'It looks like you've been in the ring with Muhammed Ali and lost!' exclaimed Gary from the PR company. 'What happened?'

'It's a long story. But it involved a ski pole and a helicopter!' I replied laughing.

Gary was not impressed. 'Let's hope your next helicopter experience at Westland's will have a better outcome!'

I peered into the toilet cubicle thinking, *I wonder if there are cameras in here?* Everywhere we went we were monitored. Hopefully not in the ladies' toilets. Westland's high-security base in Yeovil, Somerset was the site of next race!

I stood looking at the gigantic wind tunnel with a mega-high-speed fan in the middle.

'Wow, that looks a bit scary!' I remarked to Scottish skier John Clarke, my teammate in the Smirnoff Speed Skiing Team.

'It's just a like a huge pipe that wraps around itself with a mega-fan in the middle. It's run by giant electric motors. When you switch on the fan, the air flows around the pipe.' He smiled, and joked, 'This is not for the fainthearted.'

You're not kidding! I thought.

Being seriously claustrophobic, I wasn't overjoyed about being strapped onto a pair of skis inside an enclosed tube. What happened if you came off your skis? You'd be shredded by the fan, minced! I was not warming to this challenge.

The wind tunnel technician stood with clipboard in hand and bore a very large grin.

'Firstly, welcome. This is a first for Westland. Secondly, safety is our number one priority, so, please listen up, this is important.' Now no longer smiling, he continued, 'We don't have a panic button inside. But if you want to slow the fan speed down or want out put your thumb up.'

We looked at each other, all having the same thought: *Does he know how difficult it is to raise your thumb at 200 km/h?*

He continued, 'All your details, weight, height, etc. have been fed into the computer. This, plus your aerodynamic position will allow the computer to work out which of you would have won the race.'

I placed myself into the 'egg' position and motioned towards the tiny little porthole, where I could just see the technician. As I gazed at the computer screen in front of me, I heard the cluck-clicking of the giant fan starting to whirl. The noise was deafening. This was beyond scary. *What on earth am I doing? I'm too young to die. Too young to be minced!*

I have no idea how long I was in the tunnel. But when I began to feel a little unstable with the wind speed, I opted for a quick get-out. I didn't care if I came last. I am an outdoor type of person, not an enclosed tunnel type of person. The world champion Maria Bretton won the ladies' section, with British Champion Divina Galitza second, and I was placed third. I wasn't jumping up and down with excitement, as there were only three in the ladies' race. Wonder why?

***

It had been a summer of many ups and downs – none of them planned. Now it was time to prepare for the winter ski season in Europe. I only had one small problem. 'I need to be able to travel independently to all the races and training days. I need a car! I can't rely on public transport,' I informed my mum.

My mother looked at me with a twinkle in her eye. 'Yes and I need to live in a palace. Oh yes, I would also like a Rolls Royce. Thirdly, I wish leprechauns were real!'

'Mother I'm being serious. Less of the Irish!'

'Then you know what to do Iona. If you don't ask, you don't get.'

And that's what I did. Next stop was the Birmingham Motor Show. One of the biggest automobile shows in Europe. Where better to find a car sponsor. With presentation in hand and copies of all my media coverage and television interviews, I was ready. The very first exhibition stand I approached was Alfa Romeo. I introduced myself to one of the representatives and he asked me to wait. The next minute, I was sitting chatting with the Marketing Director of Alfa. *This is too easy,* I thought.

'I'm impressed,' he said, as I showed him photos and newspaper clippings of me on top of a car.

'Yes, speed skiers also train on top of cars, normally at abandoned runways,' I explained.

We talked through my proposal, and after an hour, the deal was done.

I walked out of the exhibition hall in a daze. *Was I dreaming? Did I just seal a sponsorship deal?* I was jolted back to reality as I stood at the exit. Birmingham National Exhibition Centre has one of the largest exhibition car parks in the UK, with 16,500 spaces, and as I stood looking at the sea of cars, I realized I had no idea where I had parked my mum's car. *This could take me hours, maybe days,* I thought. Maybe I could wait until everyone had left in the hope one car remained. Thankfully, a very kind roadside assistance man came to my aid.

'No worries love, this happens all the time.' After about an hour, I was happily reunited with my mother's car.

Outside of my regular training programme, I was now on call for both sponsors.

'Pleased to meet you Damon,' I shook Damon Hill's hand. Alfa Romeo had invited British racing driver Damon Hill to participate in the photographic shoot.

He smiled broadly. 'This will be a first for me. I've driven in many different situations, but none like this.'

I balanced myself on top of my car. My skis had been fixed to the roof rack and I was now strapped in and ready to go. With Damon at the wheel, we slowly took off down Fleet Street, one of London's busiest roads. The media followed closely, cameras clicking and flashing. Here I was in a skin-tight pink Lycra speed suit, perched onto top of my sponsored car with my blonde hair blowing in the wind.

This is truly bizarre! I thought. Onlookers gazed in disbelief: from buses, taxis and pavements. A cyclist wobbled and nearly lost his balance in shock. I crouched in my ski egg position, smiling at the photographers and trying my best not to lose my balance, while our chaperoning police car with its flashing lights also allowed Damon to steer through the traffic without delay. Alfa Romeo knew how to get publicity.

I gave Damon a goodbye hug and wished him luck in his racing, thinking I would probably never meet up with him again.

Not all publicity events work out as planned. Unfortunately, I seriously messed up on one that I was looking forward to. I had just picked up my newly personalized hatchback from Alfa Romeo in Maidstone, and I was driving north to an artificial ski slope to teach New Zealand cricket player Sir Richard Hadlee how to ski. I totally got my timings wrong and by the time I arrived, the media and Sir Richard had departed. I got a real earful from Smirnoff's PR agency.

Television, radio and newspaper interviews were non-stop, and with a couple of photographic shoots in the Alps, Smirnoff and Alfa Romeo were happy and waited in anticipation for the up and coming race season.

With my personalized Alfa Romeo hatchback and my Smirnoff-branded suits, skis and helmet, I was ready to hit the slopes. But which resort would I be instructing at?

Even with the financial backing from Smirnoff, I still needed to work.

More than one hundred and fifty instructors sat listening as the Director of Schools Abroad tour operator read out names, positions and the ski resort each of us would be working at. I had put in for either Les Arcs 2000 or La Clusaz, both of which had a speed track. *What if I don't get either? I'll be stuffed!* I thought.

'Iona McClure, Chief Ski Instructor, La Clusaz.'

I punched the air and jumped from my seat. 'Yes, yes, yes!' I whooped.

Silence.

The Director looked up slowly from his long list, 'Iona, we love your enthusiasm, but this is not the place.'

I sat down slowly and lowered my head, silently jumping for joy inside.

And there was more good news.

'Mother you have to stop phoning me all the time. I'm busy.'

'But you have a registered letter from the British Ski Association. I hope you don't mind, but I opened it. They have decided that you can retake your Advanced Ski Instructor's examination. They apologized for what happened. Everyone who failed can retake the exam as the conditions were so bad.'

That was good news. Little did I know then, but I would never make it back to Aviemore.

***

I stepped out of my car and took a long deep breath. *Wow, that mountain air feels good!* I was happy to be back. La Clusaz is one of those places that everywhere you look it's picture perfect. Located at the base of the Aravis range in the French Alps, this tiny ski resort offered skiers everything. Cute wooden chalets with open fires, cosy bars and restaurants, and the ski lift station practically on your doorstep. I unpacked my car while onlookers gazed at the personalized name and logos plastered all over the Alfa hatchback. *At least no one will try and steal her,* I thought.

Within a couple of weeks, my team of instructors and I had skied all the slopes, and familiarized ourselves with the local restaurants and bars – an important part of the job!

My daily routine was packed. So much so that sometimes I felt like a giant octopus who could juggle. In addition to the normal organizational activities for the ski school and instructing, I had my training routine.

'Are you crazy? Can't you see?' I screamed. 'You nearly obliterated me.' I was covered in snow from head to foot, with large chunks of ice stuck to my running suit. I was out for my daily run through the village.

'Sorry, ma'am. I didn't see you,' shouted the piste machine driver, as he carried on driving, waving his arms in the air.

I lay on the side of the road, my body shaking. If I hadn't jumped into the snowdrift, he would have driven right over the top of me. I loved my early morning runs, but training was difficult in the dark, especially at five in the morning.

'How's the training?' David asked. I was surprised to get his call, but it was good to hear his voice.

'Yes, squeezing the training in. I run before breakfast, hit the gym early evening, and do relaxation and visualization before sleep. In between, I eat and socialize. It's fairly full on!'

'Sounds hectic. How about the practice runs?'

'That is a bit of a problem. The track is rarely opened for practising. But the big races don't start until March, so I have time. There is a national race in Les Arcs in February, so maybe will aim for that as a warm up.'

'Great, let me know if you need an assistant.'

Little did I know I would be calling on him for help!

9
CRASH AND BURN

'Welcome back old friend.'

I turned to see Michael, the head of the ski school, beaming from ear to ear.

It was weird to be back in Les Arcs as a competitor and not as an instructor. The Kilomètre Lancé track took centre stage in the resort. You couldn't help but to look up in awe! This was the fastest track in the world. The one that every speed skier prayed would bring them glory.

'Yep. Feels like coming home. I've missed this place,' I said as I stared up at the summit.

'Good luck in the race. It seems to have attracted everybody. There are not enough speed courses in the world. Everyone wants to come here.' Michael waved goodbye. 'I'll be there to support you Iona,' he shouted as he strolled down the high street.

For only a minor race, Michael was right. There were more than 200 skiers who had signed up to compete. I stared across at the KL slope and closed my eyes. I felt good and focused. *What would race day bring?* I wondered. Time was short. I only had three days to prepare and I had to find a reliable ski technician to help prepare my skis and assist with my equipment on race day.

I knocked at David's door. 'David can I take you up on your offer?' The door swung open and there he stood, wrapped up like a giant Eskimo.

'Not feeling good,' he explained.

'I can see that. You look awful. I was going to ask if you'd be my technician for the race. But it doesn't look like you'll be up to it.'

'Iona, I wouldn't miss it for the world. This flu will be gone by then. Drop your skis in and I'll prepare them, and I will be at your side on race day.'

'Brilliant, thank you. I won't hug you. Maybe after the race.'

I awoke feeling a little under the weather. *Blimey, I hope I've not picked up that flu bug? Not today of all days.* It was a couple of hours later when I was trying to order breakfast, I realized that I had totally lost my voice. *Strange, this has never happened before*, I thought. But knowing I didn't need a voice to race, I soldiered on.

With my fifteen-kilo skis balanced on my shoulder and my red Smirnoff-branded helmet and poles, I walked slowly up the slope to the starting point. At the same time, I was on the lookout for David. Where was he? I tried not to let negative thoughts creep in, but I knew I needed a reliable technician to help adjust the correct settings on my bindings before I did my first timed run.

The starting point was like looking at a sea of multicoloured suits. I fitted in well with my bright pink catsuit. Everyone who was anyone within the speed skiing world was here: World Champion Franz Weber, the up and coming French superstar Doctor Michael Prufer, plus many other familiar faces. By now, I had stopped worrying about David. It was just good to be in the midst of like-minded people. It felt like community, but with adrenaline. Unable to talk, I tried my hand at sign language which, not surprisingly, no one understood.

I watched as racer upon racer took their turn. I had time on my hands, as I was way down the start list. There was still no sign of

David. I took the decision not to worry about my binding settings. They had been checked the day before, so should be good to go.

I could feel the adrenaline pumping through my body, even more so when a couple of skiers wiped out. Thankfully, they both walked away without any broken bones. I was feeling a little nervous, but this only heightened my awareness levels and helped me focus. The atmosphere was electric, the crowds were screaming, and I absorbed it all. I was in the 'zone' and ready to go.

Balancing myself with my poles, I shuffled my two-metre skis around. I took a deep breath and pushed off from the slope. As I picked up speed, I could feel the vibration of my skis on the snow and the sound of the wind in my ears. *Love this feeling,* I thought. With eyes focused on the red finish line in the distance, I remember crouching lower in my 'egg' position for better aerodynamics, when suddenly my right ski came off. Shocked and stunned, and without thinking, I put my right heel down to slow myself. As I did this, I realized that it was the wrong move: especially at 100 km/h.

The next second, I exploded into a human catapult with arms and legs swirling out of control. As I tumbled down, streams of thoughts rushed in. *Oh help, I'm going to die! Who will look after Toby? God if you're real, help!* For 1.5 km kilometres, I plunged out of control, crossing the speed track at over 160 km/h.

Then there was silence. I came to a grinding halt. *I can breathe, I'm alive!* I felt numb all over. I slowly half sat up and saw fragments of exposed bone protruding from my right leg. Then everything went black. The rest of the day became a blur. I drifted in and out of consciousness. I vaguely remember at one point watching two doctors talking and pointing at several x-ray images. I strained to see. *Wow, that looks bad!* It looked like someone had randomly thrown several pieces of bone into a pile. *Where was my leg?*

Twenty-four hours later, I opened my eyes. My body felt different. Yes, I was bruised, and I could feel the friction burn marks on my back caused by my rubber suit, but my right leg felt like it was no longer part of me. The door creaked slightly and in walked two white-coated men.

'We've put you back together,' said the taller of the two, with a gigantic smile. 'It took us eight hours. But we did it.'

I couldn't speak. I just stared at them. Frozen.

'You didn't break your leg, you shattered it! Into nine pieces. Both the knee and the lower tibia separated. I suppose the lesson is not to fall at 160 km/h!' They turned and walked towards the door. 'We'll come back tomorrow and run through your recovery programme.'

I sort of smiled and said thank you.

If you do break your leg, then the best place to be is in Albertville, as it is renowned for its pioneering orthopaedic surgery. I was in the right place, but in a bad situation. Now I was the proud owner of a long metal titanium plate and 23 screws in my right leg. The bionic woman!

I kept replaying the fall in my head. Over and over. Trying to make sense of what had happened. My position had felt good, I had been focused, then bang! I was on one ski! I lay there peering out of the window. *What now?* I thought. *Will I be able to ski again?*

Just then, I heard a knocking at the door. 'Surprise!' It was a group of ski instructors who I used to work with, laden with flowers, chocolates and teddy bears.

'Talk about going out in style, Iona. You don't do things in halves, do you?' said George.

We laughed and chatted for an hour, and then somewhere in between the talk I must have just dozed off. When I woke, the room was quiet. But I felt someone in the room. I turned to see speed skier Michael Prufer sitting on the visitor's chair just staring at me. Michael was a real charmer. Not only was he kind and compassionate, but he was also a true gentleman. We had recently been out on a couple of dates. And I knew that I could easily fall head over heels for this guy. But I kept stalling. It just wasn't the right time!

'That was one serious blow-out Iona. You're blessed to be in the land of the living.'

'Yep I know. And now you're looking at the bionic woman.' We both laughed. It was good to talk through what happened. We discussed theories on how and why, but never did come up with a final verdict.

'You're going to be off the circuit for a while. I'll miss you, but I'll call you when you get home.' Michael leant over and kissed me on the cheek, then walked to the door. 'I know it's going to be difficult, but stay out of mischief.'

There was a full-on stream of visitors. What surprised me enormously was the amount of people who were genuinely concerned about my health and well-being. I was truly overcome by their love. I know that prior to my accident, I had been somewhat self-absorbed. Life was all about me: which meant I didn't have many close friends.

Day two, and I waited for the surgeons to return. I waited and waited.

Was I dreaming, or could I really hear my mother's voice in the corridor?

'Where's my daughter?'

I braced myself. With her winter cape flowing and sheepskin hat on, she flung open the doors and launched herself towards the bed.

'Careful Mummy, careful of my leg,' I cautioned, as she went to give me a giant bear hug.

'You cannot keep doing this to me Iona. You're going to give me a heart attack.'

'Hi Mummy, good to see you too! Who told you about the accident?'

She explained that while watching BBC television sports channel, there was a news flash stating British speed skier Iona McClure had fallen at 100 mph and was undergoing a lifesaving operation.

'Iona, I was stunned! I telephoned Gary from Smirnoff. And here I am. They flew me over immediately.'

I had already received flowers and a large funny-looking stuffed dog from Smirnoff, but was overwhelmed by their generosity in getting my mother over. Our chat was interrupted when one of the two surgeons poked his head around the door.

'This is my mother, doctor.' They shook hands and he perched himself on the corner of my bed.

'Is it good or bad news, doctor?' I asked.

'I think you already know what I'm going to say.' He tried to smile. 'The good news is that you're alive. The bad news is that you probably will never ski again or compete in any sport.'

I couldn't quiet comprehend what he was saying. *That's impossible*, I thought.

'The bottom line is that you will have a limp, and you may need to have a knee replacement in the next couple of years.'

Just throw it all at me!

10
CRUTCHES AND MORE

I am naturally a loner and like my own company, so the endless days of lying flat, looking up at the ceiling gave me time: time to think. *Why do I feel so at peace with everything? I shouldn't. I should be angry. But I'm not!* Even when the surgeon told me 'no more sports', I had this feeling that this all had a purpose. If you'd asked me the day before what would be the worst thing that could have happened to me, it would have been this. So why did I feel at peace with this?

The one definite was that my life would not be the same. In a split second, everything had changed.

Recovery was long and drawn out. After three weeks in the Albertville Hospital, and a stream of visits from well-meaning friends, I was flown back to the UK accompanied by a nurse.

The Royal Gwent Hospital in Newport, South Wales became my home for the next couple of months. Only a thirty-minute drive from our family home in Pontypool, it meant my mum could visit regularly. My father, who now lived in Cyprus, visited occasionally and always arrived with a huge box of chocolates, which he then proceeded to eat by himself. Apart from not sharing my chocolates, he was supportive and eager to help in any way he could. Sadly, Daddy had his own struggles to deal with. He was now going through the final stages of a second divorce. Probably what happens when you marry your wife's best friend.

My mum was my rock through this and visited almost every day.

'Here you go. More press coverage,' my mother had an armful of newspapers both national and international. 'Anybody would have thought you'd won that race, not fallen!'

'Funny, ha ha!' But she was right, I had been bombarded by journalists since my return. People seemed to be more interested in life-threatening experiences than victories. But Smirnoff were happy. In their view, all press was good press.

On top of the publicity, I also had some strange requests. One of them was from the community on the island of Iona. They had read about my accident and wondered if I would do a sponsored hop with crutches around the hospital to raise money for them. As I had only arrived two weeks earlier, I thought they were very optimistic about my hopping abilities, and chose to put the request on hold.

Physiotherapy was painful. There is are no words to describe it, bar one – torture. My leg had been in a straight cast for so long my knee refused to bend.

'Stay still and don't move a muscle,' said this massive Scottish nurse who was holding something that resembled a chainsaw. 'We need to cut the cast off.'

I looked on in horror. Suddenly I had no control over my breathing.

'Nurse she's hyperventilating.'

'Okay quick, get a brown paper bag and stick her head out of the window.'

Before I knew it, I had a bag over my mouth and my trolley had been wheeled backwards so that my head was protruding halfway out of a window. *Blimey, I think I'm in the car park!*

'Today is the day, Iona,' Nurse Jane announced as she waltzed into my room. There was never a dull moment when she was around. Her medicine was jokes, pranks and laughter.

Today was the day I would stand upright with the aid of crutches.

'Okay, I can do this. You don't need to help me.' I was determined to stand without assistance. Wow! I was standing. But I felt so weak! It had been only 8 weeks since my accident and I had dropped nearly 12 kilos in weight. All my muscle had just vanished. Now I looked like a stick insect on crutches!

A couple of days later, I was ready to venture home.

'Good news Mummy, you can pick me up on Friday.'

The phone went silent.

'No, I'll pick you up on Saturday.'

'Why?'

'No reason, just busy.' And my mum hung up. How odd. I knew how eager Mum was to get me home, yet now she was delaying it.

Saturday arrived. I sat in my wheelchair at the entrance and watched as a large white Rolls Royce pulled up covered in white ribbons. *Looks like someone just got married. Maybe they had an accident?* I thought.

'Surprise! Surprise!' my mother leapt out of the back of the Rolls Royce.

'Wow! For me?' I squealed in delight.

'I'm not buying it for you. But I did think you should go home in style.'

Tears of happiness rolled down my cheeks and we hugged.

With my injured leg stretched out on the leather seat, I made myself comfortable.

'What's with the white ribbons?' I asked the chauffeur.

He laughed. 'I came straight from a wedding. No time to take them off! Saturday is the only day the Rolls comes out of the garage.'

Home we went! But to what?

11
SNAKE ALERT

Going home to our little Welsh cottage was exciting, especially as I was reunited with my dog, Toby. But my euphoria soon disappeared. Life became tough. Being back in familiar surroundings brought me down to earth with a thud, with the realization that things were never going to be the same. It was almost as if I had lost part of myself. I felt like I had been stripped of my identity.

I was unable to go upstairs, so I slept in the living room. I could do nothing but read and watch the television. I surrounded myself with all my old books such as *The Power of Positive Thinking* and every 'how to be happy' book I could find. I needed to find my purpose.

Every other day I was at physiotherapy: this included being plugged into muscle stimulation machines and painful knee exercises. Within a couple of months, I was able to bear weight on my injured leg. I was still on crutches but a great deal more mobile, to the point that I was also able to drive, which gave me the luxury of being independent. But I had nothing to really look forward to. It was as though my life was on hold!

Then the wait was over! Out of the blue, I received a phone call from a film producer. 'Iona, I would like to talk to you about co-producing and presenting a "learn to ski" video.'

I hesitated. Maybe it's a prank call. Randell went on to introduce himself as an independent producer who represented Virgin Videos. Not one to look a gift horse in the mouth, we met the next day and then spent the next couple of weeks sorting out contract details. It was a done deal!

Making the video was a real test – but a good one. I struggled with the fact I couldn't ski but enjoyed the presenting. The month in Austria gave me a new passion for media work, especially in television, and also for writing. Having drawn up the video script, I realised I was able to do other things outside of sport. The video aptly named 'Learn to Ski the Fast Way' was my inroad into a different world.

With the video just about to be released, I found myself back home with nothing to do.

'Iona, your father is on the phone,' shouted Mum from the living room.

I was lying on the kitchen floor playing with Toby.

'Okay, give me five minutes.' I was unable to move anywhere fast.

Strange for him to call on a weekday, I thought. *It must be important.*

'Iona, I was wondering, do you want to come to Cyprus for the summer?'

I was so shocked that I didn't reply.

'Maria also thinks it's a good idea.' Maria was Dad's new Cypriot lady friend.

'I would love to, but what's the catch?' This was not normal behaviour for my dad.

'There isn't one. Just thought the change of scenery might help you.'

He was spot on – but not in the way he was thinking.

***

'Alison, are you up for another night out?' I bellowed down the phone. My sister Alison also lived in Cyprus and worked for Dad's financial company.

'Yes, but not so late this time Iona. Some of us have to work for a living.'

By day I painted, and at night I hit the clubs and bars of Nicosia. My poor father was not impressed. 'You're supposed to be recovering from a life-threatening accident but instead you're gallivanting around town till all hours.'

In an attempt to sway me away from my nightly jaunts, he took me to his local country club, which also had an equestrian centre. It was located just outside of the city of Nicosia and was surrounded by lush countryside. I sat overlooking the swimming pool, watching the Cypriot elite as I drunk my ice-cold soda.

'I heard you can ride well,' I turned to see a very handsome, immaculately dressed man.

'The wilder the better,' I smiled.

'My name is Andreas. Your father speaks so highly of you and your sporting achievements.'

That's nice to know, I thought.

We chatted for a while and agreed to meet the following day. Andreas was one of the club members, who also had a string of polo ponies at the centre, and a stunning Lipizzaner grey stallion. When he asked if I'd like to ride him, I didn't even stop to think, I just said yes. I suppose it's a bit like asking a mouse not to eat the cheese you have just put in front of him.

Alison and I sat drinking our brandy sours in the cool evening air, at one of our local haunts.

'Are you sure you should ride?'

'No harm having a go,' I said as I stubbed out my cigarette. I had also started smoking.

I galloped around the countryside, jumped old logs and worked my new friend in the dressage arena. I was in heaven. Andreas was so preoccupied with his business ventures and his polo that it felt as if Fabio was mine. Every afternoon, after a morning of painting, I would pitch up to ride Fabio. Life was good.

'Brad can you help me get my boot off? It's stuck!' I was trying desperately to get my riding boot off, but it wasn't budging. Brad was one of the grooms who looked after Fabio. As he tugged, hanging onto the sole of my boot, I leaned back against the chair.

'Great. No stop, something moved.'

Brad started laughing.

'Yes, mam was your boot.'

'No inside my leg. Something moved.'

I knew instantly one or more of the screws in my leg had been dislodged. The following MRI and x-rays confirmed my suspicions. The horsey and dancing activities had unfortunately loosened many of the screws from the main plate which was fixed to my tibia.

The orthopaedic surgeon stood looking at the scans, 'Sorry Iona, but the only way forward is to remove the plate and screws. This also means months of intense physiotherapy. And no riding and no dancing.'

I stayed in hospital for five days. The operation was only partly successful. I had somehow managed to snap the heads of eighteen screws, so they would now be a permanent fixture in my leg. Now it was back to physio training.

Joanna, my physiotherapist, sensed my downward slide. 'You're normally so bubbly Iona, this is just a slight setback. God will have a plan for you in all this.'

'Blimey! He has a very strange way of doing things.' I half smiled. 'I think his plans for me have been derailed.'

Joanna was adamant that good would prevail.

'Why not come along to one of our Christian gatherings? You'll make new friends and have a good time. No one will pressure you to do or say anything you're not comfortable with.'

So I went along. And she was right. I felt comfortable and not threatened in any way. There was no judging or asking weird questions. They were kind, compassionate and funny. Three times a week I met up with this amazing group of people. We sang worship songs, we read and studied the Bible together, we listened to amazing speakers telling us about Jesus. We went on weekend retreats into the Troodos Mountains. This was a totally new realm for me. If all they said was true, then it would open up a very different world for me.

'I think I'd like to go and study theology, Daddy.'

He looked over and raised one eyebrow.

'Is that really what you want to do?' He went back to reading his newspaper. I could see he wasn't convinced. 'Iona, sometimes you can be very impulsive and obsessive about things.'

I knew he was right. I can become so fixated on something that logic goes out of the window. But that wasn't going to stop me!

After two weeks of phone calls, it was obvious that I had no chance of enrolling into any of the UK Bible Colleges. I didn't have the right entry requirements. The day I decided to stop my new quest was hard. I was disappointed and feeling miserable. That evening I stayed home. Daddy and Maria had gone out for dinner. *Maybe I will watch a movie. I need some escapism!* I stood in the lounge, balanced on one crutch and leant forward to switch on the light by the TV. Bang! In less than a second, I was thrown across the room. I felt the electric current run through my arm and down my bad leg. I lay in a heap crying and holding my leg. I sobbed uncontrollably. It wasn't just the fact that I'd been electrocuted, it was everything. I was depressed and battered.

'God this cannot be happening. You need to step in and help me here?' I screamed. 'Please help me!'

Nothing! Absolutely nothing!

Then suddenly I could hear the phone ringing.

'Iona are you okay?' It was Alison. 'I just had this feeling I should call you!'

Was this an answer to my prayer? I wondered.

'No, I'm not I've just electrocuted myself. But that's so freaky you called!'

'How did you electrocute yourself?'

'I went to turn one of those old lamps on with wet hands and the next minute I was flying across the room.'

'Do you want me to come over?'

'No, I'm not good company. I'll open a bottle of wine and drown my sorrows.'

The next day, with a small hangover, I packed a small suitcase and drove off into the mountains. My father owned a beautiful house half way up the Troodos Mountain in a picturesque village called Lania. When I wanted time alone, this was the place to chill out. The house was a historical building that had originally been a wine press. It was surrounded by enclosed courtyards, with orange and lemon trees. Absolute paradise. Just what I needed.

Except on this particular trip, I got zero sleep. The first night I woke up suddenly with a feeling that something was in the room. I sat up and could not believe my eyes, at the bottom of my bed, lying across the duvet was a very large snake. I launched out of bed totally forgetting about my recent operation. I fell over my crutches, screamed and hopped out of the room as fast as possible.

I bolted the bedroom door and remained in the living room until morning.

'Daddy there's a snake in the house,' I screamed down the phone.

'Not possible. I have never seen one.'

I explained that I hadn't been drinking and I wasn't hallucinating. I don't think he believed me.

'Okay, I will send some men to check it out.'

Two big sturdy-looking Cypriot men arrived shortly after the call. And found nothing.

'That's impossible. I saw it. It's in there somewhere,' I said as I pointed back towards the bedroom, in the hope that they would take another look. They smiled, but had this expression that said 'crazy English lady', and they left. I stayed for another couple of days, but wasn't convinced our new resident had left, so I returned to the safety of the city. And some much-needed sleep.

Life now was a bit different, as I was unable to horse ride or dance. Instead, Alison and I started frequenting the more sophisticated bars. Here I was introduced to Jed, a French Canadian who worked for the military and was representing the United Nations. We hit it off immediately and would meet up most evenings, and also in the mornings for coffee.

'Jed, I have my dad's car tonight. Why don't we try that new restaurant you mentioned?'

'Great but I'll have to sneak out for a couple of hours. I'm supposed to be on call and stay at the barracks. But yes, let's do this. Pick me up at 7 p.m.'

As Jed and I drove along the main highway, heading out of the city, from out of nowhere I saw a large four-wheel drive heading out of control towards us. I tried to swerve but before I knew it, the other car had rammed into the bonnet of my dad's Pajero. I did an emergency stop and wrenched my neck badly. I looked at Jed. He was visibly shaken, but okay. What on earth had happened? I sat dazed.

'Iona, I have to go.' Jed opened the passenger door and leapt out.

'What are you doing?' I screamed.

'Call the police. But remember, I wasn't here!'

And he ran across the road and disappeared into the bushes.

When the police arrived, the trauma of what happened had set in. After being checked out by the paramedics, I was put into the back of the police car. I gazed out of the window at my father's wrecked car. *He's going to kill me!* I thought. I could feel the tears welling up.

I sat in the inspector's office, chewing my fingernails. I had got an all-clear on the breathalyser test. Now I waited.

'We've called your father. He is on his way.'

I explained to the inspector that my dad had a fierce temper, and that by tomorrow morning he'd also have a murder investigation on his hands. He got my drift!

'What have you done to my car?'

I looked at the inspector with eyes that said, 'Help me!'

'Stop, stop, stop Mr McClure, your daughter is lucky to be alive.'

My father stopped dead in his tracks. 'What do you mean?'

'The guy who hit your car was five times over the legal limit. He couldn't even stand, let alone drive. If your daughter hadn't swerved, the other car would have gone right through the driver's door. And your daughter would not be here, alive and well.'

My father came over and gave me a massive hug. I winked at the inspector as a thank you. Walking away, I did feel bad. Bad because I had lied about being on my own.

Jed and I carried on dating for another couple of weeks, but after the car accident I just felt that our relationship had changed. We both did. It just fizzled out.

It had been six months since I'd left the UK and life just seemed rather miserable. To top it off, Maria was always finding fault with every move I made.

'The neighbours are talking Iona. We know what you get up to,' Maria said, red faced and angry. 'There has been a UN jeep outside this apartment on several occasions. If you want to stay here, then I'd prefer no men in the apartment. Is that clear?'

'It's one boyfriend and he came for coffee in the middle of the day.' I wasn't going to tell her that Jed and I were no longer together. I glared at her and she did the same back. I would say I got on with most people, but Maria was a different story. I was beginning to feel like a caged animal. It was time to move on!

12
PENNILESS

My dad also agreed that it was a good time to return home. As the plane descended into London Heathrow, my emotions were mixed. I enjoyed spending time with my dad, when Maria the Rottweiler wasn't around, I was physically stronger and I had made some amazing Christian friends. On the downside, I think my father was disappointed with my nightly antics, his car was now a write-off and Maria and I would probably never talk again. On top of this, I had no idea what I was going to do with my life.

Our family home never changed. It was always good to walk back in through the door and feel like you'd never left. I had no money coming in, and was aware that I needed to start work, but just kept putting it off. I was still on the media rollercoaster and still very much in the limelight. The *Daily Mail*'s Ted Blackbrow, ranked as one of the finest news and sports photographers, had followed and supported my skiing career from the very beginning. Soon after I returned, he had come to the house to take some more shots and to do a follow-up story. In addition, I was also one of the nominees for the BBC Welsh Sports Personality of the Year Award 1987. There was always something happening, either with the press, television or radio. But I knew I was hiding behind all this media attention and not facing reality. I needed to find a job, so that I didn't eat into my savings.

Christmas came and went. My leg was now much stronger, and I began to seriously consider going back into competing. I would lie awake at night thinking about what sport I could compete in. I felt like a nobody, and I wanted to show the world I was a somebody. Competing not only gave me an identity, it also gave me a purpose, a reason to live. But in what? For me skiing was still a possibility, but maybe it was time to move on and do something different.

A door opened when a friend introduced me to a local flat race trainer. After a couple of rides on his race horses I decided, with the small amount of savings I had left, to splash out and buy a thoroughbred race horse, with the view of becoming a jockey. Now armed with a new passion, a goal and a purpose, I threw everything I had into finding the right horse.

'He's beautiful, Iona. What's his name?' My youngest sister Geraldine had come home and was wanting to meet the new member of the family.

'His stable name is Benjamin and his racing name is Iona's Boy.'

'When will you race him?'

'He's still only a baby. I need to get riding fit and I have to get a licence.'

Benjamin was a stunning bay with a white patch on his head. Even though he was young and very green to ride, he was eager to learn. Which made two of us!

I was now training with a local Welsh trainer Dale Green.

'You need to ride with shorter stirrups Iona, or you won't be racing,' explained Dale as he gave me a leg up.

As the months went by, I was finding it virtually impossible to get into the jockey position, and when I did my knee would lock up. My knee was not playing ball. One of the most embarrassing moments was when I had been invited to ride out at a well-known racing stable just outside London. At 5.30 a.m. we were all aboard our horses. I was in a line of twenty other horses and work riders. I was on a little chestnut filly who was leaping all over the place.

'Remember, these horses are priceless. If I see anyone with their feet out of their stirrups, you'll wish you'd never been born,' shouted the head lad as we headed in single file out of the yard onto the main road.

After thirty minutes, the pain in my right knee was so excruciating, I thought I was going to faint. Thankfully, I got back to the racing yard without any incidents, but I was unable to move. My knee had locked completely. *Shit! How am going to get off?* All the riders had dismounted, and I sat there. *I need a plan.*

When no one was looking, with my good leg free, I threw myself forward onto the mare's neck, which meant I now had the momentum to swing my locked leg over, so I could clear the saddle. The poor horse leapt to the side in fright and I nearly lost the grip on her reins. Everyone was so preoccupied, only one jockey saw my new dismounting manoeuvre. He didn't react. He just looked at me as if I was a real idiot.

As I travelled back to Wales that day, I accepted the fact that flat racing was not a realistic option for me. That evening my mum and I opened a bottle of wine, and I relayed the day's horsey adventures. We laughed and laughed. Actually, we laughed so much we were crying. I could not remember the last time I laughed like this.

A couple of days after my jaunt at the racing yard, and knowing I was back to square one, life turned even more serious.

'We need to talk, Iona. You may not like what I'm going to do!' My mum very rarely sounded serious, but I knew from her voice she was not messing. 'I've decided to sell the business and the cottage and move back to Henley-on-Thames.' Henley was where Alison and I were born. My mum had previously talked about returning.

'I'm looking at buying a one-bedroom apartment overlooking the Thames.'

'That makes me homeless.'

'It looks that way. But you knew this day would come.'

I sat feeling sorry for myself and contemplating what else could go wrong with my life. I knew this was a good move for my mum. I just felt numb.

Now I needed a job *and* somewhere to live. After a few phone calls, a good friend offered me a job in their local ski shop in Cardiff, which allowed me to rent a tiny bedsit and bring in a small wage. It felt like the end of an era. Now I had to face reality. It all looked fairly grim.

During this time, I was also approached by HTV television to work as a freelance sports presenter. The workload was fairly limited, as I covered all the minority sports such as women's football and rugby. So, I kept the two jobs running side by side. Eventually I wanted more!

'Mummy, I've decided to move to London. I have an interview with the BBC and feel positive I'll get it.'

'Iona that's a risk.'

'They are looking for a lady to work alongside David Vine on Ski Sunday.'

'Wow!' said Mum.

'It's my dream job!'

Knowing that I would go through a process of interviews, I also applied for a telesales position in central London to keep the cash coming in.

I loaded my car up with all my valuable possessions and set off to London. I moved in to small bedsit in the suburbs. I have never been a city person, but I knew this was where the action was, and if I wanted to make it in television where else would I go?

But first, I needed to get money in. Telephone sales is not my thing, but it was a job.

'This guy is an absolute crook. He's lying to the general public.' I blurted out to my new friend Neil, who always sat next to me at work, 'It's underhand and illegal.'

'Iona you will get us both sacked. Be quiet,' Neil said as he kicked me under the table.

I leant over and whispered in his ear, 'That won't be a problem as I'm resigning.'

Within one week, I was jobless again. But on the upside, I had met Neil. Not only was he very handsome, with his dark curly hair and big blue eyes, he was a sportsman – an extremely talented rugby player. He definitely ticked some of the boxes. A couple of weeks after leaving the job, we started dating. I had also, unfortunately, persuaded Neil to leave his job. Now we were both out of work.

Unfortunately, my BBC recording session hadn't gone quite to plan.

'Iona, try and not get so excited, as you tend to screech,' said the Sports Director. I was in a studio doing a voice-over of the previous weekend's Ski Sunday races. I did several takes, but I could tell I was not impressing him.

'Thanks Iona, we'll call you.' We shook hands.

I knew it was a no-hoper. In front of the camera and presenting I was fine, but commentating on a race… Not so hot!

The money was disappearing, and there were no signs of breakthrough with television jobs. I had never been so broke. I sat in my bedsit in Croydon, perched on the window overlooking a very neglected garden. *How can a person go from having everything to having nothing so quickly?* I lamented. The final straw came when my car was repossessed. I felt like a criminal.

That same week, my father flew in from Cyprus and he invited me to join him at the Royal Oversees League Club for lunch. We hugged. It seemed like such a long time since we had seen each other. The restaurant was stunning, with its white starched linen and silver candlesticks. Even the waiters looked like they walked off a film set.

'Tell me, how is your new job is going Iona?' my dad asked.

I was unable to answer. I stared down at my napkin, as my eyes started welling up with tears.

'Not good. I resigned and now I have a grand sum of five pounds to my name.'

He looked at me in disbelief.

I knew what he was thinking. *Yes, my daughter is a failure.* He looked shocked and rather stunned. I knew that to a certain degree my drive in everything I did was to obtain praise and recognition from my father. *Could this day get any worse?* I wondered.

Lunch whizzed by and as we said farewell, he handed me some money. 'When you find yourself a job, I will expect to be repaid.'

Dad being Scottish, this came as no surprise. But this was the lifeline I needed. Feeling emotionally broken but relieved that I could survive for a couple of weeks, I went in search of another job. I do recall asking God to step in and point me in the right direction. And bingo! I was offered a sales position with the prestigious St James's Club. I thrived in this environment and it meant I could begin earning again and getting my life back on track.

During this time, I had also been contacted by a specialist orthopaedic company, Steeper Clinic. They offered to design a special leg brace for me, one that would fit around my knee and would be directly bolted onto to my ski boot for stability.

'If this brace works, I could make a comeback into skiing.' I had called Belinda, one of the instructors I used to work with. We had stayed in contact since my accident.

'Tell me when you're trying it out and I'll come and watch.'

I was due to participate in a photographic shoot at one of the dry ski slopes in London, with all the national press later that week.

'Yes, would love the support. This will be my first time skiing since the accident two years ago.'

The constant media interest seemed to fuel my dream that there was hope. It was a very weird sensation walking around in ski boots. The brace was comfortable, and I did look like the bionic woman. It was a beautiful sunny day and I could hear the birds singing. I stood at the top of the slope and pushed off. I had no idea how my leg would react. I made a turn to the right, easy. I made a turn to the left, not so comfortable. By the time I got down the slope, I knew this was going to be a no go. I smiled at the cameras. Thankfully, I wasn't there to chat, it was just a photo shoot. I drove home in silence.

'Sorry I couldn't make it. How did it feel Iona?' said Belinda.

'Nope it's a no go! The brace was amazing and did its job. It's the broken screw heads in my tibia. When I put pressure on the front of the boot, the metal bits dig into my leg.'

'Sounds painful. Don't worry you'll find your thing soon enough.' Belinda said goodbye and hung up.

I loved working at St James's Hotel, but I wanted to focus on a position in public relations, so within a couple of months I had landed myself a new job. I was now PR Manager for two London Embassy Hotels. Neil and I moved from our scruffy Croydon apartment into a posh flat near Earl's Court, and for a year we both worked hard to get some finance behind us. Then came the day to move to pastures greener.

I had been contacted by a new public relations company in Peterborough, Cambridgeshire. They offered me a salary that I could have only dreamed of. Neil and I packed up and ventured into the unknown world of neighbouring Lincolnshire. We fell in love with the countryside, and after six months of settling in bought a four-bedroom house in a quaint town of Deeping St James. Neil also had picked up a good job. So, along with his rugby and my passion for my new job, plus our two new kittens Brian and Pickles it was *perfecto!*

But was it? Was this how my life was to be?

On the outside all looked great, but deep within I felt there had to be more than just this. I felt like I was just going through the motions, while carrying an emptiness inside. I remembered the experiences I had when I was doing my sports visualization and relaxation. It was one of peace and stillness; it gave me the ability to live in the moment and experience a presence that I believed was God. *Maybe I should look at Buddhist mediation,* I thought. So, I set aside an hour each day to practise, thinking this would help!

It didn't!

'Why not try crystal healing? It's amazing,' said Graham. He sat surrounded by all these coloured gems that came in all shapes and sizes. As the Art Director of the PR company I now worked for, it seemed okay that he was a bit quirky.

'Here you go, give this lady a ring. You won't regret it.' Graham handed me a business card. What did I have to lose?

I lay on the floor with my arms stretched out, encircled by hundreds of crystals. It felt as though I was about to exorcized.

'Just empty your mind and let the crystals do their thing.'

Judy was an older lady who looked like a Romany traveller. She had rosy cheeks, wore colourful clothes and carried an array of crystals around her neck, ears and wrists.

'Your aura is beautiful, Iona.'

I had no idea what she was talking about but could except the 'beautiful' bit. I left with many new acquisitions: crystal necklaces to keep me calm and at peace, crystals that were to be used when I mediated, and crystals to place around the house. In addition to my crystal fetish, I started to meet up with tarot card readers and delved deeper into astrology. I felt a little like Indiana Jones in search of the Holy Grail, and an answer to life's secrets. But my searching only led to dark blind alleyways.

However, it wasn't all darkness on the horizon.

13

MALABAR TO THE RESCUE

One year later, January 1991, I sat in a sophisticated café in London's Covent Garden with Susie. She worked for one of the biggest advertising agencies in the Middle East, and was looking for extra staff for the PR department she ran. Susie was tall, glamorous, and wore a lot of make-up.

'You have the right profile for our agency. It just depends on whether you are prepared to relocate to the Middle East.'

My father had given my CV to his next-door neighbour in Cyprus, who also worked in Bahrain, and this meeting was the result.

Susie was intense and seemed to rarely blink. 'You don't need to give me an answer now. But I will need one in a couple of days.'

She stood up, grabbed both my shoulders and kissed either cheek, smiled, handed me her card and marched out. That was some lady!

This was an opportunity, but was it the right one? I knew it would be a challenge – and that was an incentive. Neil, on the other hand, was unwilling to give up his job. The last time I had asked him to do this, we'd both ended up in a financial hole, so yes, I could understand why he was a little reluctant. Eventually we agreed that I would go on my own, as this might be another dead-end job.

My first couple of weeks could best be described as traumatic. Upon arriving at my new job, the Art Director was the only one who smoked, so I warned him that under no circumstances should he give me a cigarette if I ever asked for one. I had started smoking seriously in art college and then quit when speed skiing came on the scene. And then had started up again in Cyprus.

Seven days into my new job, I asked, 'Peter can I just take one cigarette?' I smiled sweetly, as I hung over his desk.

'I will keep to my promise and say no, Iona.'

I was so stressed out working alongside Susie, I just needed a helping hand – in the form of a cigarette. 'Peter, if you don't give me a cigarette, I promise you I will break every bone in your body.'

He looked at me as if to say, 'Are you serious!'

'Okay, take it!' He handed me the whole packet. My first week was not going as planned. If I was to choose a movie character to describe Susie, it would be someone like Cruella de Vil from the film *101 Dalmatians*. Within fourteen days I had resigned, but the office manager declined my resignation and offered to move me into a different department. I took on the role of Account Director for some of their multinational companies. Work became fun, but my sporting pursuits hit a crossroads.

Within six months of settling in Bahrain, I had joined the Twin Palm Riding Stables. A month later, I had bought a little Arabian horse called Karim. He was a chestnut gelding with a feisty streak. I knew Karim was not an easy horse – he came with issues and had a serious attitude – but he was mine. As he had only just been backed, I had work to do, but I needed a project outside of work, so he was the perfect horse. In only three weeks of training, Karim and I were beginning to bond and I could see he was beginning to trust me. Then came a call that I was not expecting.

'Iona I am so sorry but we have some bad news.' The manager of the Stables was on the phone. 'Karim died last night from colic.'

I felt like I had been hit over the head by a sledgehammer.

Neil was with me when the news came through. He had just arrived on the island to try and find a permanent job. He put his arms around me.

'I am so sorry Iona, I know you loved that little horse.'

I couldn't speak. I just felt numb.

It was a couple of weeks before I ventured back to Twin Palms. Anki, who ran the equestrian centre, was kind compassionate but also very firm.

'You need to get back riding. It's the only way you'll get over this.' She smiled and gave me a hug. 'And I have just the right horse for you.'

Malabar was a beautiful grey Anglo Arab who had a reputation for misbehaving and bucking his riders off. I loved challenging horses like this and it wasn't long before I was smitten with him. The only problem was that I had spent most of my savings on Karim and could only afford half of Malabar. You can't do a lot with only half a horse! I was heartbroken.

'Daddy, remember when I was eleven you promised to buy me a horse if I passed all my exams.'

'Remember it well. Why?'

'I know I failed one exam but I'm only asking you to buy half a horse, not a whole horse.'

He couldn't stop laughing. 'I'm sure there is some logic in this argument.' To my utter amazement, he agreed.

From here on in Malabar and I were joined at the hip. The weekends comprised showjumping competitions and cross-country events. Being able to compete again was a dream come true. Life was looking even better when Neil proposed. I didn't hesitate, it just felt right.

But we almost got divorced before the big day. We were leaving my boss' house after dinner, and as we walked down his driveway I could see something white and fluffy in the flowerbeds. It was the tiniest puppy I had ever seen – and the cutest. I picked him up and put him in my jacket pocket.

'There is no way on this planet you are bringing that home,' shouted Neil. 'I'm not letting you in the car until you put it back where you found it.'

Well, I thought, *that's an easy decision.* 'No puppy, no wedding.' And the problem was solved.

I named him Beano, after my favourite comic, and he became the centre of my existence, next to Malabar. My weeks consisted of working long hours, showjumping, watching Neil play rugby, topped off with plenty of socializing.

***

A major turning point in my career came when I was given the Rothmans Williams Renault Formula One account. The first six months were intense, especially as I was preparing for our wedding at the same time. I had unknowingly dropped down to 46 kilogrammes and looked like a skeleton. The hours were long, but I loved my new role, so by the time our Big Day arrived, I was exhausted. It was a full church wedding, with a reception down at the Bahrain Marina. My father, mother and sisters all attended, and we celebrated into the early hours of the morning.

Unfortunately, when we got to the honeymoon suite I could not stop throwing up. I was horrified. If this was food poisoning, then all the guests would be sick. However, this was not the case. After a trip to the doctor, all was made clear. I was physically exhausted and totally run down. My body had just reacted.

I sat looking at Seeman, my boss, as he tapped his pencil on his desk nervously. 'This is difficult Iona because I don't want to lose you.'

Oops am I getting fired, I thought.

'Rothmans have asked if we would release you to work on their Formula One account for the Middle East. Which means you have to drop all your other accounts.'

'Are you serious, that's awesome!'

'Unfortunately, there is one catch. You will need to relocate to Dubai.'

I loved Bahrain, but it was beginning to feel a little claustrophobic. It was a no-brainer! Thankfully, Neil agreed.

14
IN THE FAST LANE

Walking along the pit lane watching the mechanics and their teams work on the cars was fascinating. This was truly another world for me. I had travelled over with twelve journalists who were all now settling in to their five-star hotel. The Italian Grand Prix was my debut into the sport.

'Iona, we will introduce you to the drivers and then you can walk around and get your bearings,' said Nick.

I had worked with Nick now for about a year. He had worked for Rothmans for most of his working life and was a true professional when it came to public relations. In a funny kind of way, we were similar; he was also intense and rather obsessive.

Branded from head to toe in Rothmans Williams Formula One gear, we stepped into the team's marquee. It was a hive of activity. Everybody seemed to have a job to do. We sat at one of the tables and discussed the agenda for the next couple of days. Just as my coffee arrived, I saw Damon Hill walk in. I smiled broadly. Last time we'd met, I was wearing a pink Lycra speed suit and he was driving me around the streets of London. I never expected to meet him again. Nick introduced us. Damon shook my hand.

'Yes, we've met before.'

I could feel myself beginning to blush. I was praying that he'd not mention the pink suit and our adventure down Fleet Street. He didn't.

'Great to see you again Damon.'

'Welcome to the team, Iona.'

Then in a flash, he was gone. It wasn't until the next day that we met Damon's teammate Ayrton Senna in the 'meet the drivers' briefing for the journalists. I remember clearly Ayrton saying that there was one part of the San Marino track he didn't particularly like. He chatted with our Middle East journalist and then left to prepare for the race. He seemed a little subdued but that was understandable, as his close friend Roland Ratzenberger had crashed and died the day before in qualifying.

I stood near the start line. The noise of the engines was an adrenaline rush in itself, without the cars even moving. I watched on the monitor as Senna led the way. Then, without warning, Senna's car was in pieces with smoke blurring the camera's vision. The crash was fatal. We had been with him a few hours earlier, and now he was gone. Everything seemed to happen so quickly. It was a tremendously sad day, and one that I will never forget. I could not understand how two drivers could die at one event. Was this normal for Formula One? Unfortunately, the next race, in Monaco, saw driver Karl Wendlinger crash and end up in a coma. I was now beginning to consider an exit plan. *One more race,* I thought.

But at the Barcelona Grand Prix, the dark clouds lifted when Damon won the race for Rothmans Williams and no life-threatening accidents occurred. For the next couple of years, I worked alongside Damon, David Coulthard and Jacques Villeneuve. Out of the sixteen F1 races held each year, I would attend ten. It was a glamourous lifestyle: one of five-star hotels, private helicopter rides, business class flights and beautiful venues with celebrities. It was stressful but good.

***

I was watching television, but I could tell Neil was anxious.

'You'll burn yourself out. Too much travelling, drinking and smoking.'

'It's all part of the job. Don't fret, I will be fine.'

'We just don't see each other,' he was downing a large pint of electrolytes after a workout. He was right. We very rarely crossed paths, and my health was suffering again. Neil had become one of the rising stars on the Dubai rugby scene and was now also on the Gulf Rugby Sevens team, which meant he trained most evenings and played rugby at the weekends. While I was either at an F1 race or at showjumping during the day, during the evenings I was usually down the stables. We were both consumed with our own passions. I knew we were drifting apart.

'I've decided to go to Ireland for a break,' I told Neil.

'I thought we were having a holiday together?'

'Next year would be better. I have the opportunity to train with Olympic showjumper Jack Doyle.'

My showjumping had suffered with my workload and travelling schedule. I really wanted to do well in jumping, and this would give me the boost I needed. I had also received a sponsored horse, a warmblood called Pina Colada, and I really wasn't doing her justice. After six months in Ireland training with Jack, I had a different mindset. I was eager to go back into sports on a professional level. I wanted to be the person winning, not the one helping to promote others. Surprisingly it was the next F1 race which opened a new door for me.

***

I stared out over the racetrack. Every time I came back to San Marino, I remembered that tragic day.

'You look so sad?' I turned to see a smiling couple who were arm in arm drinking champagne.

'Memories,' I replied.

We were standing in the Rothmans Williams Renault sponsorship box waiting for the qualifying sessions to start.

'Nick was telling us about your speed skiing and showjumping accomplishments.'

I laughed. 'Remember he's in public relations. He'll exaggerate!'

Laura and Sam were sports promoters and were always on the lookout for potential talent. I thought an F1 race was a strange place to look, but afterwards I found out that they had been invited by Rothmans and were here on a purely social basis.

When I returned to Dubai, I was surprised to receive an email from Laura. She and Sam were coming to Dubai and asked if we could meet. 'After you opened up and told us your dreams of going back into professional sport, we felt that we could help you.'

Laura, Sam and I were sitting in one of the many five-star restaurant in Dubai, enjoying the most amazing French food. I tried not to get over excited but with half a mouthful of food, I did struggle to swallow. I wondered why they wanted to help me.

'You're a natural athlete Iona. We have some ideas we would like to discuss with you.'

Within two weeks of our get together, I was at the Brands Hatch racetrack for a one-day assessment with a Formula 3000 racing driver. Based on my love of speed, Laura was adamant that I should try out motor racing. So here I was.

I drove around the track in a rally car with my new race friend sitting next to me, with no instructions except to drive as fast as possible. I had no problem with that. But on one of the corners, I accidently put my foot on the accelerator instead of the brake and nearly lost control. But my examiner, not knowing my mistake, looked rather impressed as I accelerated into and out of the corner and managed to keep all tyres on the road.

That afternoon, I also had the opportunity to drive a Formula 3000 car. Again, I was to drive as fast as possible. Each lap would be timed. I loved the speed and the way the car accelerated. I had done a fair amount of indoor karting, but this was on a different level.

I jumped out of the car. 'That was fun,' I shouted. Philip my examiner wasn't the most talkative, so I had no idea what he thought.

'Iona, give me ten minutes. I need to write out your assessment.'

My heart was thumping in my ears and my legs were still a bit jelly-like, but I was smiling. Judgement time. Philip handed me a slip of paper. I didn't have a chance to look at it, as Laura and Sam suddenly reappeared, they had been watching from the grandstand. Laura took the paper from my hand.

'Not bad, not bad.'

What does that mean, I thought?

I grabbed the slip and read the bottom line: 'Has a great deal of potential. Excellent.'

Laura and Sam were on a roll.

'Okay, we'll contact some racing teams in the USA. We'll be in contact.'

For months I heard nothing. Then the phone call came.

'We have a team that may be interested. But you need to go to the USA for another assessment.' Laura, as always, was upbeat and excited.

'I will need to look at my work schedule. I'll get back to you.'

Before we finished, Laura reminded me of the consequences of my decision.

'You will have to resign your job, forget about showjumping and you need to think about Neil.'

I knew that I would have to leave the Middle East – and probably Neil – and venture out on my own into a very different world. I kept thinking, *Am I passionate about motor racing? Is this the sport for me?*

While I was debating whether motor racing was for me, I decided to take a break and return to Ireland. For the next eight weeks, I threw myself into a busy schedule of showjumping – competing in indoor and outdoor competitions around Ireland, under the guidance of trainer Jack Doyle. I needed this time, even though Laura and Sam were waiting for an answer. I wasn't sure if I wanted to give up on my equestrian pursuits.

After much soul searching, I made the hard call to not pursue the racing driver option. I know I was ready for a change, but I didn't feel that this was it.

15
DIVORCED THEN DUMPED

I was out on Murphy, my Irish-bred showjumper. I had bought him a year earlier from a friend who had given up competing. He was a handsome, stocky, liver chestnut gelding with an unusual flaxen mane and tail. In other words, drop-dead awesome! As we walked around the Dubai Equestrian Centre, the sun was coming up and the birds were singing. *I should be happy,* I thought, *but I'm not.* I had everything. A high-powered job, beautiful home, horses and a husband. *So why do I feel so empty inside?*

Was it time for a change? After five amazing years with the Rothmans Formula One Team, I felt it was time to move on. I was tired and worn out; I was absolutely drained.

Nick refused to accept my resignation. 'Take a couple of months off and think about it.' He was kind and caring and I knew he was concerned. He smiled and pushed the letter back into my hand. 'You just need to take a long holiday.'

But my mind was already made up. I was going to work freelance. I knew this was a risk, but it felt right. Having specialized in photography at art college, I decided to turn my hand to photo journalism.

Within six months, I had regular work with two of the largest equestrian magazines in the UAE – *Race Week* and *Al Adiyat,* which was run by Dubai Central Military Command. I now had more time for my showjumping and felt like the oomph I'd lost had now returned. Alas, this did not overflow into our marriage.

We sat outside the coffee shop perched on the steps of the equestrian centre, holding our steaming coffees. This was a morning ritual after jumping lessons with trainer Trevor. Same group of ladies every morning: Tracey, Wendy, Anne and Mehta.

'Iona you know you have a very serious admirer. Trevor is smitten,' Tracey said.

I looked up and laughed, 'I'm a married woman.'

'So, what!' said Wendy.

'To be honest Neil and I are more like brother and sister.'

'Wow! Does that mean no sex?'

'Yep, it's a bit like that.' I could feel myself blushing.

'Girl you need to get that sorted. With a body like yours, what a waste,' Tracey was smiling.

We were all laughing.

'It's complicated!' I said.

I got up and walked to my car.

As I drove away, I got to thinking. I knew deep down Neil and I had come to an end, but I didn't really want to acknowledge it. I knew also that Trevor was igniting feelings that I hadn't had for a very long time.

For the next couple of months, I enjoyed the flirting, but knew I was heading towards dangerous ground. One night after drinking too much, I ended up having to stay at the Dubai Equestrian Centre. I suddenly awoke at 3 a.m. *Where am I?* I thought. I was on the sofa in Trevor's apartment. I rushed downstairs and headed to the car park. Just as I was coming around the corner, I saw Neil drive up.

'Where the hell have you been?' he yelled.

'Had a couple of glasses of wine and fell asleep. Sorry.'

Neil was angry, but I think also relieved that I was in one piece. That night made me realize that I had to decide one way or the other. Neil was a really awesome guy, but I wasn't in love with him and I also didn't want to hurt him. I lay awake pondering how I was going to do this. There was no right way to tell him. It was bad timing also, as his parents were staying with us.

I took a shower and walked into the bedroom. Neil was sleeping, but barely visible, as Minky our Persian cat was draped around his head.

'Neil. I know this won't come as a shock. But I want a divorce?'

He immediately sat up, dislodging poor Minky as she flew through the air.

'Why? What have I done?'

'You've done nothing. It's just that we are more like good friends than husband and wife. We have nothing in common. I'm sorry.'

We sat in the kitchen and talked, but there didn't seem to be a solution.

Later that day I packed two suitcases and left, with Beano in tow.

'No mother, I've moved out. I'm staying with a friend called Trevor.' I spoke to my mum at least three times a week.

'Poor Neil. He must be traumatized,' she scolded.

'He'll be fine. I'm going to sign over my share of the house to him. It's the least I can do. And he's got the cat.'

'Iona, this is all so sad.'

'And who exactly is Trevor?' My mum sounded very irritated.

'Just a good friend,' I lied. I had fallen head over heels in love with Trevor, but he wasn't the reason why I left Neil. Our relationship had morphed into a platonic one.

So, within a six-month period I had a new job, I was getting divorced and I had a new boyfriend. Trevor and I had one thing in common, showjumping and our love of horses. He was a trainer, and I wanted to compete.

But within nine months, I could feel a change. I had a feeling he was seeing someone else, but I wasn't sure. The crunch came when we travelled with the Dubai showjumping team to spend the summer training in the UK. We were now at the English showjumping venue, Hickstead, one of the most prestigious events on the calendar. I came back to my hotel room exhausted. The team had done really well, but there was a point in the day when it looked like the team were going to be arrested. We had been sitting under the shade of some trees watching the different classes, and the Dubai riders were smoking their shisha pipe. Without us knowing, some bright spark had reported the Dubai team to the judging committee accusing them of doing drugs. After hours of explaining that shisha was just flavoured tobacco, the boys were reinstated back into the competition.

As I lay on the bed giggling at the misunderstanding, out of the corner of my eye I spotted an envelope on the floor by the door. I opened it and stared at the contents in disbelief – Trevor was finishing with me. I sat bolt upright. *What!* I felt like I'd been punched in the belly. I'd had a feeling something was up, but I was not expecting this. I sat on the bed dumbfounded. I knew he was due back later that evening, so I went into autopilot and started packing. I didn't want a confrontation. There was no way I could stay on and help the team. Working alongside Trevor would not be an option. I needed somewhere to stay. But where could I go? There was only one person I wanted to be with right now and that was the rock in our family, my mum.

'Mum, can I come and stay for a bit?'

'I will need to speak to Barbara. I'll call you back.' My mother was now working for the author and writer Barbara Cartland and was living at her beautiful home in Hatfield, Hertfordshire.

Barbara agreed to my visit, on the condition I looked after her dogs when she went on holiday to Scotland next. I agreed. Her house was in a time warp. It was filled with antiques, family heirlooms and memories. This was where Beatrix Potter wrote *Peter Rabbit*, and I'm sure I saw a few of his relations hopping around the gardens.

I struggled with my emotions. It had been a long time since I'd experienced rejection. It hit me hard! Did I really love him that much? No, I don't think so. So why did I feel like my insides had been ripped open? I really needed to sort my head and heart out.

***

I was back in Dubai. It was just Beano and me. I'd had to leave Malabar in Bahrain due to his health problems and I had sold Murphy just after leaving Neil, as I was struggling financially. I also made the decision to not relive the memories of the Dubai Equestrian Centre and moved my equine pursuits to the Dubai Polo Club.

'Iona, I have a string of polo ponies to be exercised. Are you interested?' asked Harry. He had his own financial business in Dubai and knew I was keen to get involved in polo.

'Yep sounds good. But only in the mornings, as I have my polo lessons in the afternoon.' I buried myself in work and in my new love of polo. Trying hard not to think about my failed love life, I pushed to get my life back on track. But it was about to be derailed again.

16
THE BIG C

In the summer of 1997 my world came to a grinding halt. 'Am I talking to Iona Davenport?'

'Yes, who is this?' I didn't recognize the phone number.

'We've been trying to track you down. It's urgent. We need you to come to the doctor's surgery as soon as possible.'

My doctor had been trying to contact me before I left for the UK, but as I felt he had other motives, I ignored the calls. I was perched on the edge of the chair, listening and trying to make sense of what I was hearing.

'The test results show you could have stage three cancer of the uterus, leading into stage four. We need to check you into the American Hospital immediately for a biopsy.'

My friend Carol had accompanied me to the surgery. I had been sleeping on her floor for the last couple of months, as I was in the process of trying to find a suitable flat for myself and Beano. Carol took over and asked all the questions, while I just gazed off into the distance. *Was I in the middle of a bad dream?* The day before, I had fallen from a polo pony and broken my nose, and now I was being diagnosed with cancer.

'Do you think they could straighten my nose at the same time?' I asked.

The doctor looked up, thinking I was joking. But he could see I was deadly serious.

'I'll put in a request on your admission form.'

Four days later I was boarding a plane to London on the way to see a Harley Street specialist. My biopsy showed the cancer was bordering on stage four, so I opted to go home to England for treatment. On the plus side, I had a straight nose. Making the decision to go to London was easy after the oncologist at the American hospital stated, 'If you were my daughter, I would be sending you back to a specialist in London.'

Two days after arriving in London, I was on the operating table. My whole uterus, cervix and part of my vagina was to be removed in what they call a radical hysterectomy. This all happened so fast that I think I was unable to process how I felt. Ten days earlier, I had thought I was healthy; now my future was uncertain.

As I came around from my operation, my father was leaning over me with tears in his eyes. *Blimey I must be dying*, I thought. *My dad never cries!* He was clutching the Paddington Bear he had bought me and was looking so sad. As I peered over my oxygen mask, I could just see my mother at the foot of the bed, she was also clutching a teddy, Rhubarb the rabbit. Another one for my collection.

Reality set in pretty quickly. I now knew I could never have children, but my focus was on my future. The question was, did the surgeons manage to remove all the cancer? I stayed six weeks in the Royal Free Hospital and waited. Even though I felt like I was in limbo, I was still optimistic. My hours were filled with reading and thinking. I read books on prayer and actually started to pray, but I wasn't sure if God was really listening. And why should he?

My lovely Harley Street surgeon popped his head around the door. 'Thought I'd drop in on my way to dinner.'

'Wow look at you. Must be a special occasion,' I said.

He was wearing a black dickey bow and dinner suit.

'I have some very good news. The results are negative. You are cancer free.'

He came over gave me a hug and then excused himself. I lay there listening to the noise of the nurses laughing and joking in the corridor. *Thank you, God!*

Now that I had made it through this, I needed to find somewhere to recuperate until I had the all-clear to fly. I wasn't able to stay with my mum, as Barbara had a house full of visitors. A couple who I had met through Trevor stepped in and offered to look after me and put me up at their farm. To this day, I will never forget their kindness and compassion. My recovery was long, slow and painful.

And so was my return to Dubai. I struggled to find freelance work and got kicked out of my studio apartment because they found out I smuggled Beano in and out every day. Months went by, and then finally I was reinstated onto the *Race Week* team and was also offered regular work with the Dubai Central Military Command again. In addition, I was now working on a weekly racing supplement for the largest English newspaper in Dubai, *The Gulf News*.

Having now moved in with an American friend, Becca, life seemed to be getting back to some kind of normality. It was back into full throttle: work and play. Becca was not much of a night owl, like I was, so I mostly went out on my own. Somewhere deep down I had this belief that if I found the perfect partner, then it would somehow complete who I was. So I merrily went on a quest in pursuit of the ideal man. Night after night. My quest was not going to be an easy one. I felt like a lioness hunting for prey. However, the more dates I had the hollower I felt.

Workwise it was smooth running. It was hard work, with crazy deadlines, but good. As I specialized mainly in flat racing, I attended the big international races such as the Dubai World Cup, the richest race in the world. I absolutely loved my job and I knew I was good at what I did, but at night I morphed into a different character – one not so savoury.

'Becca, I don't know how I'm going to survive the summers here?' I admitted one day.

She knew I was going to struggle to pay the rent on our shared villa.

'Don't worry, something will turn up. Why not look at going back into public relations work for the summer months?'

Because of the extreme heat in the summer, all equestrian activities were put on hold. Which meant no work. I did action Becca's suggestion, and to my surprise was offered a consultancy contract with a property group who specialized in shopping malls. I ended up working in a very lively, fun marketing department. Here I befriended Tracey who, like me, lived life to the max and partied every night without fail.

'Iona, there's this new guy in town. He's the new Director for Property. You need to meet him.'

'Why Tracey?'

'He's smart, handsome and single. And he's Australian.'

'Sounds more like your type of man,' I chuckled.

The first time I met Jeff was in a wine bar, surrounded by very attractive air stewardesses. Every one of them seemed captivated by him and his jokes. I knew straight away that he wasn't my type. I had also heard through the grapevine that Jeff had a ten o'clock evening curfew, so at exactly ten, he would leave and go home. I was normally arriving then. So, we would be ships in the night, which simply wasn't the right criteria for a relationship. I wondered if maybe after ten he morphed into a pumpkin or something!

As the months passed, I saw Jeff on several occasions at dinner parties and celebratory events. I did try and avoid him, even though on many occasions we were seated next to each other. Our friends were determined that, one day, we would somehow connect.

One evening I was curled up on the couch watching television with a bag of cheese and onion crisps and a gin and tonic. Becca walked into the living room with a 'What are you doing?' expression.

'You must be sick. Don't tell me you've decided to stay in?'

I laughed and nearly choked on a crisp.

'I've made a radical decision. I'm too old for all these late nights. As of tonight, that's all finished.'

I took a swig of my ice-cold drink and lay back on the couch.

'But I do have one last party to go to. And that's Maureen's birthday party at the Alamo.' Maureen was the company receptionist and a real treasure. It would have been wrong not to attend. The Alamo was one of my favourite haunts. It was renowned for great bands, yummy food and its famous dwarf, who was the regular bouncer at the front door. Halfway through the evening I felt like I had enough, and sat down to watch my friends dance wildly and sing very badly. I was thinking it was about time to go home, but just as I was about to leave, Jeff sat down next to me.

'Can I join you? I don't like eating on my own and you're the only one sitting down.'

If that was a chat-up line, he's failed! I thought

'Why not,' I replied. But secretly was kicking myself. I really was exhausted and wanted out from the noise. This was not what I needed just then. We discussed work and past memories. I nearly choked on my wine and thought about making a quick exit when he told me he'd been married and divorced three times. But through all this, we laughed. I mean really laughed. Not only was he intelligent, he had bucket loads of charisma and was funny. I couldn't remember the last time I'd laughed so much in one evening.

Suddenly he stopped and looked at his watch. *Oh no, was he going to turn into a pumpkin?* I wondered.

'I need to go. Great evening. Thanks for the company.'

'Same, same,' I said. As he walked away, I shouted, 'It's my birthday next Friday. We're having a party at the villa. Why not join us?'

'Sorry no. But thanks.' He waved and left.

Blimey, what went wrong there? I wondered. This made me even more determined to stay at home and become a couch potato.

17
ENDURING LOVE

'Iona, are you awake?' Becca was knocking at the door.

'No, I'm not. Go away!' My head hurt, and I could barely open my eyes. Why had I drunk so much?

'Your mobile keeps ringing. Could be important.'

'Okay, I'll be out in a minute.' I'd left my phone in the lounge to charge. Just as I walked out of the bedroom, the phone rang again.

'Happy Birthday Iona. It's Jeff. How was the party yesterday?'

Stunned, I asked why he declined my invitation, and he explained that he was away in Egypt. To this day, I'm not sure why he hadn't explained that at The Alamo. I wondered if this could this be an Australian way of communicating.

'How about dinner tomorrow?'

'Yes,' I agreed. 'Sounds like a plan.'

Our first date was hilarious. We had dinner in a beautiful Italian restaurant, but the FIFA 1998 World Cup quarter-final was on and Italy were playing France. Our Italian waiters were unable to focus or concentrate on anything but the game. The evening's service deteriorated rapidly when Italy lost on a penalty shoot-out. This was topped off by a French party in the next room, who were busy celebrating their win, much to the dismay of our waiters. But regardless, we were both able to laugh through the evening. As we walked out into the humid, sticky night, Jeff waved his hand and summoned a taxi.

'How about trying that again tomorrow evening?' he suggested as he kissed me on the cheek.

'Yes okay, but without the football.'

From our second date, we were inseparable. Jeff had transported me into another world: a world of laughter, friendship and adventure. He made me feel special. He opened doors for me, pulled out chairs for me at mealtimes, held my hand when we walked. He treated me like a lady. I believed that men like this did not exist. And if there were any, they were a very rare breed. Jeff was a real gentleman. Looking back at when I first met him, it hadn't been love at first sight, but I know now that you don't judge a book by its cover.

'Becca, I'm going to move in with Jeff.'

She was cooking one of her many awesome dishes, while Beano ran around the kitchen in the hope of an odd scrap.

'You know what? That comes as no surprise. You guys were made for each other.' Her seal of approval meant a great deal. Becca was a dear friend.

It had been three months since our first date. Now we were embarking on settling down and creating a home. Work was still crazy with its deadlines and I was frequently working until ten at night. I had also started back exercising polo ponies. As Jeff was also a keen horse rider, we both rode out together most mornings.

Life took an unexpected turn when I accepted an offer to ride in a ladies' endurance race. It was a sport I had criticized in my writings because of the questions about lack of horse welfare, so I initially said no. But the endurance trainers, a lovely New Zealand couple, John and Wendy, kept pushing me to accept. Wendy called again: 'She was a polo pony but is now ready to do her first endurance race.'

'I'm sure you can find another rider,' I suggested.

'We've looked, but no one really bonds with her. We know you can ride horses with attitude, plus you play polo. So, you have things in common,' Wendy was not giving up. I laughed, not sure about the logic in that.

'I will come and do a couple of training rides on her and then we'll talk about the race,' I offered.

I realized almost immediately why no one bonded with this little bay mare. She took great pleasure in bucking whenever possible but normally at a gallop. On both training rides, I had lost a couple of baseball caps and she had unseated me, but I hadn't hit the ground. She was a real handful, but I was beginning to predict her moves. I also renamed her from Paradise to Paradise Lost, as every now and again she would lose it emotionally. It seemed to suit her.

I had never done 25-kilometre training rides before, and my injured knee was swollen and painful. I was not sure if I would survive the race. But after a couple of trips to the doctors and very strong anti-inflammatory drugs, I agreed to tackle my first endurance race.

The race was run over 47 km, with two circuits and a vet check in-between. Jeff was one of the crew helping me and he was in his element. I'm not sure who was more competitive, me or him. Paradise Lost was also on top form. She was loving the race so much, she was forgetting to buck, but at the half way mark she nearly had me on the ground. Crafty!

We crossed the finish line in seventh place out of fifty participants, which was awesome considering we were newbies. I was exhausted, and my knee was swollen and sore, but the success outweighed the pain. That evening I was working as a photographer at the Dubai racetrack. I was so tired I could barely lift my camera. After three hours, I was done. It was time to eat. Jeff and I went to our favourite Thai restaurant. I had my Thai green curry in front of me, and then the next thing I can remember was Jeff shaking my shoulders.

'Iona wake up, wake up.'

I had literally fallen asleep in my curry. I woke the next morning and hobbled to the bathroom. My right leg was blue and swollen, and every now and then I would get a shooting pain that felt more like an electric shock. *Oh dear,* I thought, *maybe the French surgeon was right!*

But something inside of me had been re-ignited. My passion for endurance racing increased as I was invited to compete for other top trainers. It wasn't long before I was racing in 120-km races, even with my leg issues.

'Jeff I've decided to buy my own horse for endurance.'

He looked up from his novel.

'Why would you do that? You have plenty of horses to ride.'

'Because it's all about bonding. I don't really know the horses I race.' To be successful at this sport you really needed to know your horse well. Spending time together allows you to understand your horse's personality, their potential and also their weaknesses. My passion for the sport came from the fact you were able to have the most amazing relationship with your horse – one of trust and respect. If I was going to put my all into this sport, I needed my own horse.

I bought a small pure-bred Russian Arabian called Aktash. He was spirited, with a serious attitude. Jeff also decided to buy himself a horse from the same trainer, a beautiful stallion called Sharouse. Both were stable mates and had raced on the flat for the last couple of years.

For months, our morning rides never lacked excitement. We were beginning to realize that turning a flat racing horse into an endurance racer was not that straightforward. But within a year, Aktash and I had successfully competed in a couple of international races under the banner of Great Britain. I was competing most weekends on either Aktash or riding out for John and Wendy, while Jeff helped with the crewing.

We were now heading towards competing in the longer races. The qualifying races were normally under 90 km and then the international FEI (Fédération Équestre Internationale) races were 120 km, with 160 km being the World Championship level. There were also two-day FEI rides, some covering 200 km and more. The longer the races, the more loops. For a 160-km race, you'd normally have five loops each at around 35 to 40 km. The 120 km would be four, and so on. At the end of each timed loop, you would arrive at the vet gate. The timer would only stop running when you presented your horse to the vet. You'd only do this when your horse's heart rate was below a certain rate. Too high and you're 'vetted out'. So, if you had a horse with a great heart rate, it was possible to overtake other competitors in the vet area. The other criterion was that the horse had to be sound, without any metabolic issues. After the vetting, you had a hold time of between thirty and forty minutes to rest the horse before going out on your next loop. This sport differs from many equestrian sports, in that if you cross the finish line in first, you are not the winner until the horse passes the vetting. And the horse must in the vet's eyes be 'fit to continue.'

Endurance was all-consuming. So much so that it was eating in to my work. It was 9 p.m. and I was still struggling to finish the feature I was writing.

'Jeff, do you want to go and buy some ice cream?' I knew he would never say no. He was an ice cream addict. An hour and half later he strolled back into the apartment.

'Did you make it yourself?' I hollered from my office.

Silence. I carried on typing.

'Here you go: ice cream with extras.' He positioned the bowl of ice cream down. And then placed a gift-wrapped box next to it.

I looked up to see a big cheesy grin. 'Surprise!'

I opened the box. It was a beautiful diamond necklace. It was stunning. I jumped up and gave him a hug.

'I need to send you out for ice cream more often.' We both laughed. We sat on the couch with our bowls of ice cream and curled up together with Beano.

'You really need to slow down a bit Iona,' Jeff cautioned. He was right. I was up at 4.30 a.m. every morning to ride and then working through to 10 p.m. at night. 'Why not give up on the photo journalism and concentrate on endurance training?'

In my heart that's what I wanted, but I kept hearing my father's voice, 'Remember, never rely on anyone. You must be independent.' But Jeff was one of the only men I had ever trusted, and I seriously wanted to compete professionally.

'You know you're right. If I am going to do this, I have to put everything into it.'

This decision brought some balance to our lives. I loved the endurance racing and home life was good, especially as we had now moved a to a beautiful four-bedroom villa. Just in time for the arrival of a new family member!

I had caught a little wild kitten with a butterfly net at the Dubai Equestrian Centre. I used a net so that I did not lose a body part while trying to catch it. We named her Spit, as that's what she did for the first year. We actually didn't get near her for about twelve months, as she only came out of hiding during the night. She had decided to make her home in the downstairs toilet. She was so small that she was able to live in the toilet rim! We always forewarned our guests that there was a wild kitten in the toilet. For some reason that never went down too well. Eventually, she began to trust us and became a very important member of our family, even though she would occasionally steal food, attack our friends and terrorize the dog.

With horses, dog and cat all settled, it was time for a holiday. But this was a vacation that came with a surprise twist.

18
PAINTING A TALE

Jeff and I had now been together for three years and were enjoying another holiday with my father in Cyprus, at his home in the mountain village of Lania. Normally our holidays were mixed – half business, half pleasure. Jeff promised that there would be no work meetings on this one. We awoke to another beautiful day and decided to visit a family friend and well-known artist John Corbridge. For three hours, we sat and viewed all John's new paintings. As John went to get yet another bottle of white wine, Jeff turned to me and said, 'I think I'm going to buy three of his paintings. What do you think?'

'Are you kidding me! Do you know how much they cost? They're not cheap Jeff.'

But he'd already made up his mind. After the second bottle of wine, we staggered back through the village to the house. I immediately called my dad to tell him what Jeff had purchased. My father was shocked.

'One painting, maybe, but three, wow, that's extravagant!'

Jeff stood next to the phone laughing; maybe it was the wine. We didn't normally drink in the day. But we were on holiday. I put the phone down and turned to Jeff.

'Why three?'

He walked away, heading for the toilet. He turned and looked at me and casually said, 'It's an engagement present.' Then he closed the door.

I just stood there like a stunned mullet. I hadn't been expecting that! When he finally re-emerged from the bathroom, I questioned him, 'Aren't you supposed to ask first?'

He coolly strolled up to me.

'Will you marry me?'

'Yes, yes,' I smiled, and we laughed, hugged and kissed.

Outside of planning the wedding, endurance racing took centre stage. I threw everything I had into training and competing. The early morning desert rides, the 60–80-km weekend training workouts and our gallops around the camel track were exhilarating, fun and challenging. But a storm was just about to hit our family.

We were sitting with Juan and Becca outside their quaint villa overlooking the beautiful polo fields of Desert Palms Country Club. Our horses were stabled here. After a late afternoon ride in the desert, we'd regularly pop in for an ice-cold beer before heading home. I was telling Becca that my youngest sister Geraldine had called the day before, very concerned over my mum's state of health.

'She wanted me to fly home to Ireland. I told her I was racing this weekend so I couldn't.'

'What's wrong with your mum?' asked Becca.

'She had a reaction to a flu injection. Can't be that serious!' Just then my mobile started. I took a quick look and saw that it was an Irish number, but one I didn't recognize.

'Am I speaking to Iona?'

'Yes, that's me.'

'I am calling from Waterford Hospital in Ireland. We have your mum here in intensive care. You need to come as soon as possible.' After speaking for another twenty minutes, I hung up. I felt like the world had suddenly stopped. Jeff, Becca and Juan were all just staring at me.

'They think she might have leukaemia or something similar. They recommended that I leave immediately.'

There is nothing in the world that can prepare you for news like this. Mum was only 61 years old. She didn't smoke, she didn't drink, she exercised. This could not be happening!

Two days later, I was at the hospital. By the following day, the whole family had arrived. We all sat bunched together in a tiny waiting room. My mum's oncologist came in and introduced himself.

'I am sorry, but your mother has been diagnosed with cancer of the lymphatic system.' He sat down. 'The flu injection triggered everything. It looks like the cancer has been there for a while.'

Questions were asked, but we never really got a feel of what the final outcome would be. Mum looked pale and exhausted. She had already started chemotherapy and the effects were noticeable. What did surprise me was my mother's attitude. Normally she was a little bit of a worrywart, but now her whole perspective had changed. From the onset of this illness, she was more concerned for her family than herself.

Supporting our mother was our family's priority. As we all lived in different parts of the world – I was in Dubai, Alison was in San Francisco, Frances in Zimbabwe, Geraldine in London and Daddy in Cyprus – we orchestrated a plan that meant one of us would always be at her side. Even though my parents had been divorced since I was 11, they had stayed in contact. I knew deep down that my mum was still very much in love with my dad. But she was rather shocked when he arrived unexpectedly at the hospital.

'I must be dying if you've turned up!' She was laughing. We weren't.

'Promise me you won't delay the wedding Iona,' Mum begged as she gazed out of her window. No one knew how long my mother had left. What we did know was that it was too late for a cure.

'I promise.' I struggled to hold back the tears. I didn't want to think about the future. Watching my mother disintegrate day after day was heart wrenching, but through all this it was my mum who told the jokes, it was my mum who made us laugh, it was almost like she was the one that was there for us.

'Don't look so sad Iona, God has a plan.' She held my hand and smiled.

My mother had such a strong faith. One that I did not understand. How could God let this happen and why was my mum so at peace with all this? It was my time to leave and return to Dubai as Geraldine had just flown in from London. It had been just under three months since my mother had been admitted. She was looking out at the rolling hills in the distance, looking serene and content.

'I hate saying goodbye, Mummy, but I will be back in a couple of weeks.' I tried hard to be upbeat but was struggling.

'Don't be anxious Iona, I'm going home soon. Everything will be all right.'

I gave her a kiss on the forehead and a massive hug. I left, holding back the tears, but when I closed the door behind me, I went into meltdown.

One week later, when the phone rang in my office, I just knew. I knew she'd gone. I called Jeff at work and went downstairs. As I walked into the kitchen, the garden door suddenly blew open and a large red butterfly flew inside, followed by a rush of warm wind. It was as if Mum had come to say goodbye. I stood rooted to the spot. Remembering Mum's words, 'I'm going home soon.' It wasn't her earthly home she was referring to but her heavenly one.

Ireland has a reputation when it comes to wakes. Not only do you mourn, you also celebrate. My mother would have loved her funeral and her wake. I know that sounds strange, but let me explain why she would have enjoyed it. First, we had three Catholic priests fighting over who was going to lead the service. In the end, it was divided between the three of them. Second, the wake was one that lived up to Irish tradition. At four in the morning, we were still going strong.

However, we did make one mistake regarding Mum's headstone. We had not realized that there was a height restriction on headstones, and that the very large ones were only for bishops, priests and the elite. We had ordered and erected a five-foot stone cross. Thankfully, to this day no one has ever complained, but every time we go to visit, we cannot help but chuckle as we see her headstone in the distance – you can't miss it! But you know what, Mum was larger than life, so it is fitting!

19

A SHARED MARRIAGE

The weather in Cyprus was delightful: warm and sunny with a light breeze. You could smell the strong scent of blossom in the air. Jeff and I were standing by a wishing well in the gardens of the local municipality offices, while we posed with family and close friends. The mandatory civil ceremony was simple and relaxed. This had to be the best day of my life. It was just perfect.

As the church wedding was in two days; today was about family. The family celebrations were low key, just simple and relaxing. Our ceremony was followed by champagne and Cypriot delicacies at my father's house in the mountains. We sat in the courtyard surrounded by fruit trees and lush vegetation, listening to the sound of classical music streaming in from the living room. Veronica, Daddy's new girlfriend, had cooked up an array of local dishes. It was a time of laughter and tears. Joy for our marriage, yet sadness that Mum was not present at this special occasion.

Two days later, I looked down from my bridal suite and could see our guests all waiting for the buses to arrive. We had more than eighty friends from every corner of the world joining us for the church wedding. I watched their faces as the old Cypriot school buses arrived. Normally they'd be packed with screaming children, goats and other livestock hanging out of the windows, but today they were dressed up in ribbons and flowers. I could see many were laughing. I hoped they hadn't been expecting luxury coaches.

The tiny church was located in a village at the start of the mountain trail. As I arrived, I could see everyone was crammed tightly into the pews, but all were smiling and happy. With the sun shining through the stained glass window and the smell of the flowers wafting down the aisle, it was picture perfect. Jeff stood waiting, handsome and proud, as my dad walked me down the aisle, which was so narrow I kept knocking my hip on end of the pews. Today I knew what a princess felt like, and Jeff was my prince charming.

It was the perfect wedding.

'Do you want to stop and pick up some booze?' the driver shouted back to us.

We had all piled into the school buses on our way to a mountain village taverna for the wedding reception.

'What a good idea!' everyone shouted. After a quick detour to the supermarket, the singing started. It got louder and louder. The local pedestrians stopped in their tracks as they heard and saw the buses approaching. We looked more like a busload of teenagers out on our first holiday.

I squeezed Jeff's hand, 'I think we're lost. Are you sure we are in the right village?'

Jeff found it highly amusing, 'Yes it's the right village but where's the restaurant?' he laughed.

My dad looked stressed. 'This is a disaster. Whose bright idea was this?' he complained.

Instead of taking us directly to the restaurant, the drivers dropped us above the village, so that we could walk down through the cobbled streets to the restaurant. It was a comical sight watching smartly dressed adults negotiate their way through the winding village streets. The drivers had forgotten to point us in the right direction. Every street looked the same. It looked like a maze!

Then we heard a scream. I turned and saw Carol Mather, my friend and wife to horse trainer Bill, collapse to the ground. The stiletto heel on her shoe had snapped right off.

Oh that's not good, I thought.

Eventually we found our venue. The champagne and yummy canopies helped us forget about our challenging hike through the village. But within minutes, there was another commotion.

'Look what you've done to my dress!'

I peered over the top of turned heads to see my Matron of Honour and best friend, Becca, looking down at her beautiful lilac dress which was now covered in red wine.

'Sorry, sorry, my hand slipped,' my dad's friend Colin was frantically trying to make amends.

'Have another champagne, Becca. It will come out in the wash,' Jeff intervened. He wasn't always the most diplomatic!

We danced, we did the conga, we joined in the plate-smashing dance, we sang, laughed and talked. The food seemed to be never ending. Dish upon dish kept arriving at the tables, while we were serenaded by a guitarist. I really didn't want this day to end.

My dad was sitting next to me and getting a bit fidgety. 'I hope Jeff doesn't mention you are wife number four,' he whispered during the speeches.

'Daddy your track record is almost the same as Jeff's.'

'Iona I'm thinking of your image,' he laughed.

I knew it wasn't my image he was concerned about but his own – Scottish pride. But I did have a giggle. It was a fun-packed evening, which ended with a group of Cypriot dancers setting fire to parts of their clothing and then running around frantically as one of the 'volunteered' guests would try and put the fire out. A strange custom!

The ride home was also entertaining. We were flying down the narrow mountain tracks at full speed, swaying from side to side. Our guests were all happy campers and sang loudly as we rolled from side to side, heading back to the hotel.

'Jeff do you think our driver has been drinking, he's all over the road?'

'Yes, he was at the bar with the other driver all night enjoying free drinks.'

'Maybe we should say a prayer?'

Jeff laughed. I was being serious! However, we all arrived safely, ready to fight another day.

It was two down and one to go. With the civil ceremony and the wedding over, it was time to celebrate Jeff's fiftieth birthday. As all the guests were staying at the same hotel, it was a doddle to organize an evening party. We didn't have to worry about the daytime activities, as Jeff had made his own plans.

'Iona, remember I've organized workshops all day with consultant architects and engineers.'

'But it's your birthday!'

'I had a choice, the wedding day or my birthday.'

I smiled, 'I understand!' remembering our phone conversation. A couple of days prior to our wedding, Jeff had phoned from Dubai, sounding a bit sheepish. At first, his tone caused me to wonder if he was getting cold feet. But no, Sheikh Mohammed wanted a presentation before a certain date, and it coincided with our wedding celebrations and honeymoon. As most of the architects were friends and guests at the wedding, they were more than happy to make a few extra dollars on holiday.

With the civil ceremony, church wedding and birthday celebrations behind us, we embarked on yet another adventure. I sat in the airport lounge looking at the storm clouds rolling in. Jeff was deep into one of his science fiction novels, while I kept reliving the memories of the past ten days. I wouldn't have changed anything. However, I couldn't say the same for the flight!

'Did we just get struck by lightning?' I cried, as I dug my nails into Jeff's hand (a regular occurrence when we were flying in turbulence).

'Yes, big time!'

I'm not a great flyer in storms and nor was our British pilot, who actually swore when he apologized to the passengers. Air traffic control had managed to take us directly into the storm. We were thrown around like a ball in a washing machine. A great way to start our honeymoon. We were on our way to Paris. Our honeymoon had been reduced to a couple of days, as we were now scheduled to fly to the USA for five weeks, so that Jeff could liaise with architects. On the positive side, we were now going to be flying first class to America with all expenses paid.

***

Paris was awesome. But it was quick – over in a nanosecond! Next stop America.

I sat on the veranda overlooking the beach as the early morning mist rolled in. Jeff had just left for meetings and I had the whole day to myself. For the next five weeks, we would be in Balboa Island just outside Newport Beach, California, staying in a small but quirky apartment. This wasn't the honeymoon I was expecting, but what the heck, it was going to be relaxing. My days were spent walking, reading, lounging around in trendy cafés and sunbathing. The evenings were spent not only with Jeff, but also with all the architects. I was beginning to realize that I had to share Jeff. And not only with humans but also with machines!

It was 2 a.m. and I could hear the ringing of the fax machine and the noise of paper streaming out onto the bedroom carpet. *Not again!* I thought. I was beginning to see how and why Jeff had three ex-wives.

'Jeff, are you awake?'

'Yes.'

'You're going to have to make a decision. It's either me or the fax machine you sleep with. I can't handle this every night!'

The Dubai office had ignored Jeff's requests and were still faxing documents at about lunchtime, Dubai time, which just happened to be 2 a.m. in the morning in California. I think it was a close call, but after careful consideration, the decision was made to unplug the fax machine during the night.

When we did get the opportunity of spending time together, Jeff wanted to shop. He loves shopping. I don't! But he specialized in developing shopping malls, so I suppose this was to be expected. On one of our trips, we stopped off at a designer superstore. While Jeff browsed through the store, I planted myself near the front entrance for a quick getaway and to read my book. To my surprise, Jeff appeared in front of me with a trolley full of clothes.

'You picked those for me?'

'Yes, so why not go and try them on?' he smiled and pushed the trolley towards me.

'If it makes you happy, why not!' And with that I strolled towards the fitting rooms. An hour later I emerged, found Jeff and gave him back the loaded trolley.

'Which one do you want?' he asked as he guided the trolley to the cashier.

'All of them!' I replied.

He never did that to me again. And yes, he did buy them all.

Five weeks went by in a flash. But it felt like a lifetime since our wedding. To make up for our lack of honeymooning, we stopped in Hong Kong on the way home. As we touched down, we were informed by the pilot that the city had a red alert weather warning. Sightseeing was out of the question. There was only one other thing to do, and that was shop. Jeff was in heaven.

20
SOMETHING'S MISSING

'Oh, I missed you my little man.' I could see Beano bounding towards us as we opened the front door. He launched himself into my arms. *I love this dog so much*! I thought. It was good to be home. Spit glared at us across the room as if to say, 'Don't expect me to greet you like that!' We knew it would be at least three days before she would grace us with her presence.

'Welcome back Sir, Madam,' Prakash came running out of the kitchen with a wooden spoon in his hand. Obviously cooking up another delicious chicken curry. Prakash was our houseboy, or should I say man. He was nearly the same age as Jeff. Prakash took care of the pets, the house and us. We saw him more as a member of our family – an important one who kept us in line. I did wonder sometimes if we worked for him.

We touched back down into Dubai running. Jeff submerged himself into work, while I started the horses back into full training.

Most mornings, Jeff and I left the villa at 4.30 a.m. By the time we reached Desert Palms, Aktash and Sharouse were saddled and ready to go. Every ride was memorable. The dunes stretched out before us, with camels silhouetted on the horizon. The sun would just be coming up as we set out onto our desert tracks. Every now and then we'd feel a cool breeze as we dropped into a valley. The desert was alive with cacti, lizards, snakes and the odd wild cat or rabbit. We walked, trotted and cantered. Each day was different. Some days it was a long fast ride, others just a plod. Then, every third day we would join the stream of polo ponies as they were exercised around the polo fields.

***

'Hello! Hello!'

We turned to see the owner of Desert Palms, Ali Bawardy, speeding towards us on one of his golf buggies.

'I've been wanting to speak to you both,' he said.

'I have the perfect villa for you to rent.' He pointed to a villa which was under construction, not far from our stables. We knew the day would come when he was going to ask us, but we felt it would be too much like living in the patent place of the horse world. Not for us!

'We would be interested on one condition . . .' Jeff and I had discussed a plus for the villa but doubted Ali would agree. 'We'd say yes if we could have two grass paddocks for our horses.'

Ali looked at us with an expression that showed that he might agree. 'Let me think about it.'

Jeff and Ali shook hands.

Six months later, we were sitting on our veranda overlooking our horses grazing in the paddocks below. The house was open plan, with a massive garden surrounded by bougainvillea. With the option of having our horses out on grass, we had also invested in a couple of new additions, a handsome grey American gelding called Bear and a grey stallion known as Desert Dancer. It was time to move up a level.

I was unsaddling after a morning ride, when the polo manager Robert Thame stuck his head through the stable window.

'Good morning. And how are the desert rats today?' he asked.

'Robert you may have just answered our prayers!' I exclaimed.

He looked surprised.

'We were wondering what to call our endurance team. Thank you, now we know.'

As he walked away, he shouted, 'You know me always here to help.'

The newly named Desert Rats Endurance Team now consisted of four horses, two professional grooms and a race crew headed by Jeff. Our horse box got branded with a new logo and name and we were all fitted out in Desert Rats baseball caps and polo shirts. We were now ready to take on the world of endurance.

During the next six-month racing season, it was rare for us to miss a race. With the younger horses racing in the qualifying races of 40, 60 and 80 km, and with the more experienced horses racing in 120 or 160-km races, our weekends were full. And on a free weekend, I was normally invited to race for either John and Wendy, or an American trainer Emmett Ross. I was blessed to be doing what I loved.

Training the horses was exciting and challenging. It would take a minimum of two to four years to get a horse qualified for the international events of 120 and 160 km. I always put my success with endurance racing down to two factors: a great horse and a superb crew of people helping. We normally had three to five crew members helping us. Jeff would drive next to me for most of the race, with music booming out of our four-wheel drive, while one of the grooms would be rushing to hand me bottled water for pouring over the horse's neck to keep it cool. The desert racing was fast paced, and this rolled over into the vet checks – it's a bit like having a pit stop in rally racing. In the holding pens, each of the horses' heart rate was monitored, they were fed, their legs were iced, and they were massaged. A good crew was swift and professional – and that's exactly what we had.

***

Just look at that sunset! I said to myself. Beano and I were on the roof overlooking the garden and the desert dunes. Jeff was about to go off travelling again. Actually, his schedule was so busy that most months he would only be home for ten days at a time. Today I felt melancholy. Why? I shouldn't. Life was almost perfect. But it felt like there was something missing. The night before Jeff left on one of his trips, I quizzed him on how he viewed life.

'Don't you ever get the feeling there has to be more than just living and dying?' I said to Jeff.

'I don't really think like that Iona.'

'There must be more. Life doesn't make sense without a purpose. What's the point? Why bother doing anything if we're all just going to end up six feet underground?'

'Iona, this is a bit deep. You're asking the wrong person.'

'Then who's the right person?'

Silence.

I had restarted reading the Bible every day and praying. It was like reading a history book about a great guy, and when I prayed it never felt like anyone was really listening. But I kept at it. *Maybe I should venture out into the unknown*, I thought. But what?

Dead on 6 p.m. every day it was gin and tonic time; sometimes earlier at the weekends and after a race. Today it was 5.30 p.m., it was the weekend and I had my G and T and Jeff had his rum and coke.

'I've decided to go and see a tarot card reader.'

Jeff looked surprised but didn't comment.

'I heard that they can tell you not just your future but give you pointers on what you should be doing with your life.'

'Are you sure that's a wise move, Iona?'

'I'm sure no harm will come to me.'

The tarot card reader was a lovely round lady who chuckled to herself now and again. After forty minutes of having my cards read, I was fairly blown away by what she knew about me, but I had this nagging feeling that something wasn't right. Her apartment just made me feel uneasy. Is that normal? I'd heard about sick building syndrome; maybe this was one of those cases. I did go back a couple of times more, but on each occasion, as I left I was beginning to doubt what I was hearing. A couple of months later, I tried out reiki healing and when that yielded no results, I went back to crystal therapy.

'Iona darling, what has Aktash got around his neck?' asked Jeff as he was helping me feed all our stable cats, of which we now had about ten.

'That's a crystal to keep him calm.'

Jeff turned and came over to give me a hug. 'Don't tell me I've married a crazy crystal lady.'

'It will work. Just you wait and see!'

It never worked!

Smirnoff Speed Skiing Team, Iona and Scottish team mate John Clarke

Taking time out to relax on the slopes in France

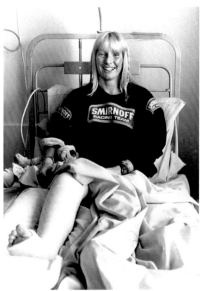

One month after her accident recovering at the Gwent Hospital in Newport South Wales

Malabar and Iona showjumping most weekends   Working as a freelance equestrian photo journalist in Dubai

Iona racing Gaziza Larzac

Iona with her father Bob and sisters Alison, Frances and Geraldine celebrating Bob's 70th Birthday in France

Iona and Desert Dancer winner of the Irish 160km two-day race

Jeff and Iona on the Gold Coast with Shiraz, Be Bop
and Lady Bella

Iona on her race horse Benjamin

Member of the Smirnoff Speed Skiing Team

Iona and her husband Jeff

Working with Rothmans Williams Renault F1 Team

Iona and her sisters Alison, Frances and Geraldine

Morning walk in Dubai with some of the Rossely rescues

St David's Convent girls out riding. Iona on her favorite 'Ginger'

Racing as part of the Welsh Ski Team at Pontypool Dry Ski Slope, South Wales

Iona as Chief Ski Instructor with her team at Les Arc 2000, France

Celebrating her win at the Salomon Gull windsurfing
and ski Ironman competition

Windsurfing Instructor and watersports manager in Corfu

First speed skiing race at La Clusaz France

21

SKI DUBAI

'Do you fancy coming on a business trip to Spain, Iona?'

'Yes, that might work.'

The summer of 2002 was upon us and the horses were having their annual training break.

We sat in a coffee shop in Madrid with a gentleman called Malcolm from Acer Snowmec. While Jeff and Malcolm chatted, I took sips of my steaming hot latte and gazed out of the window at some of the best-dressed people on this planet. I felt like a hillbilly compared to them. But then again, I felt the same way in Dubai. So, what's new!

Jeff was busy drawing a picture on a white serviette. I peered over to check out his artwork.

'That looks interesting. What is it?' I said.

'It's a ski slope – or I should say a fridge in the desert.'

I laughed.

'Malcom has the technology to create snow within an indoor structure,' explained Jeff.

'So?'

Jeff smiled, 'We're looking at building a ski slope in Dubai.'

At this point I thought they'd both lost the plot and continued to gaze at the free fashion display on the street outside. Jeff loves his work and always says he's never worked a day in his life. As a property developer, he oversaw developments from assessing the land to commissioning the architects and engineers and monitoring the whole process until completion. Mainly on master plan communities, shopping malls, hotels, golf and marine resorts. Now he was trying to add a ski slope in the desert to his résumé. Crazy or what?

Three years later, I realized I hadn't married a madman. Jeff and I were standing alongside Majid Al Futtaim in Ski Dubai at Mall of the Emirates, watching the first snow being pumped out onto the slopes at -8°. It was 10.00 p.m. and we all huddled together with Majid's entourage, amazed at what was happening. I now take Jeff very seriously when he gets a serviette out and starts sketching.

22
IRISH PRIDE

I opened the couriered package. Finally, I had my Irish passport. I had been racing under the banner of the British Endurance Federation for the last couple of years, but before my mother had passed away, she'd had one request: 'Iona why not apply for your Irish passport and then you can compete for Ireland. Do it for me and your grandfather.'

My grandfather Dennis Stanley was the only horseman in our family, and I knew my mum wanted to keep our equine passion under the Irish flag. This move was reinforced at one of the international races, when Irishman Major Brian Dunn, a friend and Fédération Équestre Internationale (FEI) Official, suggested I should seriously consider the switch, as it would give me more opportunity to compete in world events.

Thinking this would be an easy process was a mistake.

'Hello, this is Iona Rossely, I was just ringing to see if you received all my race results?' This was my third time in trying to get a response to my application as a member of ILDRA (Irish Long-Distance Riding Association).

'Yes, we did, but are you sure you want to change? Maybe you should think about it a bit more,' said Sian. I couldn't understand what she wanted me to think about. Was I missing something? Maybe I wasn't of the right calibre to become a member. Maybe it was my

English accent with an Australian twang that didn't fit. It sounded like Sian would like me to just disappear. Funnily enough, while we were having this conversation, I was also decorating our Christmas tree with my free hand, but as I was talking to her, our thirteen-foot tree suddenly shifted and started to fall. I leapt up but was not quick enough. The tree landed across a glass-topped table.

'Oh, what the . . . !' I yelled.

'What did you say?'

'Nothing, it's the tree! Maybe we should chat another time.' I hung up.

I collapsed in a heap and cried, surrounded by glittering silver balls, red tinsel and a fallen tree. Was this an omen, I wondered? These were not only tears of frustration, but tears of sadness. I missed my mum so much. Would this emotional pain ever go?

Eventually, after months of waiting, I was enrolled as a member of ILDRA, which meant I was now eligible to race under the Irish flag.

Jeff was cooking on the BBQ, and I was busy creating an Iona salad, when my mobile rang. It was Kevin Crooke, one of the officials from ILDRA.

'Good news Iona, you're shortlisted as one of the six to represent Ireland at the World Equestrian Games in Jerez, Spain.'

'That's awesome. Thank you, Kevin.'

'We'll be in contact with all the details.' Kevin said goodbye.

I stood frozen to the spot and cried tears of joy. My mum would have been so happy. Jeff was elated. I was jumping for joy. I finally got the opportunity I was waiting for.

***

The whole experience of representing your country at this level is overwhelming. The opening ceremony in Jerez was mind-blowing. Thousands of spectators were screaming and waving as we paraded around the stadium. There were 48 countries and more than 500 competitors. I was marching alongside some of the best equestrian riders in the world. The atmosphere was electric. I had qualified for the 160-km race three months earlier on a French-bred horse owned by trainer Stephane Chazel. Gadgy was a big bay mare with some serious attitude and was an experienced campaigner. This was going to be an interesting race.

'Oh, I hate that noise,' I moaned and rolled over. It was 2 a.m. and time to get up and get to the venue. Race day was upon us, with a start time of 4 a.m.

'That's one serious storm,' Jeff was peering through the curtains. 'It hasn't rained all summer and today it does, how unlucky is that!'

As we drove through the driving rain, it was hard to be positive: 160 km in a storm like this is not ideal for man or beast. When we got to the stables, our crew was there as well as Gadgy's owner and trainer, Stephane. We stood with Gadgy trying to keep her calm as we listened to the thunder and watched the lightning and the torrential rain. She was understandably nervous, and she wasn't the only one.

Stephane looked worried. 'This is not good.'

Thanks, great words of encouragement, I thought.

As Gadgy was a fairly excitable horse, we agreed to let the front runners go and leave five minutes after everyone else. I knew we had all day to catch up and I didn't want her to fizzle out at the start.

Armed with head torch and fluorescent tubes on my saddle, we were ready. It was 4.00 a.m., pitch-black and the race was on. Within the first ten minutes, I passed 1998 World endurance Champion Valerie Kanavy on foot, leading her horse. She didn't look happy! Her horse had lost its racing pads, plus a couple of shoes in the knee-deep mud. We then came across a rider in a bush and two loose horses heading back towards the start. It was chaos. This was more like a battleground than an endurance race. In addition, Gadgy was behaving like a total goofball because of the storm. It took everything I had to control her.

We were fortunate only to lose one shoe on the first loop, but as the day went on, I could feel Gadgy losing steam. This was not like her. At the 120-kilometre stage, we had a reinspection. They were concerned about her metabolic state and, sadly, as her heart rate was slightly erratic, we were vetted out. Later we found out that she had piroplasmosis, which was why she had an elevated heart rate.

The 160-kilometre race proved a real challenge for all 150 riders. In the end the weather conditions won the day, as 58 per cent of the competitors were either vetted out or had wisely retired. But it was not all sadness. There was a silver lining for the Irish team, when Charles successfully completed the 160-km course. This was enough to send us all into party mode. Can't keep an Irishman down for long!

23
GINGER NUTS

We'd just finished an 80-kilometre training ride out in the desert and were now off to a flat racing stables in Sharjah to look at a horse that had been recommended.

I strolled up to the stable.

'Stop! Don't get too close. He doesn't always like strangers,' shouted the head groom.

'I thought we were looking at a horse, not a Rottweiler?'

'It's best if we bring him out to show you.'

Jeff and I watched as his groom spent the next twenty minutes trying to get a head collar on him. He was a beautiful-looking animal, a red chestnut gelding, lean and strong. But with way too much attitude.

Paradiz had been bought from Russia as one of the best racehorses over long distances. Sadly for him, the UAE's races were shorter in distance, so by the time Paradiz was fuelled up and powering ahead, the race had finished, normally leaving him in the middle of the other runners. A friend and well-known horse trainer, Satish Seemar, suggested that we have a look at him, as he had potential to become a great endurance horse. He had the stamina and attitude.

He came flying out of the stable with his ears flat back and teeth ready for any poor soul who was nearby. His regular jockey came and put him through his paces, so we could get a better feel for him.

'Wow, he moves beautifully, but personality wise he has issues!' I commented.

Jeff agreed.

We went away to think about it. The question we had to ask ourselves was did we really want a horse like that?

For some unknown reason I kept getting drawn to the wild and rebellious animals that nobody else wanted. Deep down, I felt that I could give them a better life. One that would utilize all their potential and make them happier. Maybe it was also because I saw a little of myself in them: a rebel, never wanting to follow the rules! Could it be that like attracts like?

I picked up my mobile as I paced up and down outside our stables.

'Where is he? You should have been here two hours ago,' I shouted down the phone. Patience is not one of my strong points.

'We can't get him in the horse box,' the groom sounded distraught.

'How did he travel to the races in the past? On roller skates?' I was not amused.

Three hours later, our Russian thug, now renamed Paris, was in his stable next to his four new teammates. He didn't look impressed, but time would tell. He probably just needed a holiday! I stood in front of his stable looking at a horse that had the best facial expressions I had ever seen. All of which included his ears, tongue and teeth. *What on earth have I let myself in for?* I wondered.

A month later . . .

'How's Paris doing?' Jeff was eager to have a ride on him.

'Well he's different. Firstly, he thinks he's the boss, so he is a bully, secondly never ever go near his back end, he's mega-quick with his back legs, and thirdly he likes to use his teeth, and not for eating food.'

'Okay, maybe I will wait a couple more months before I ride him.'

***

I was cantering at a steady pace. The weather was hot and humid, not ideal for a 160-km race in the desert. There were over two hundred riders from all over the world competing in World Championships. It was good to be on home soil, but not in these conditions.

'What a beautiful horse,' I said, as a young girl came past with a stunning chestnut mare with a flaxen mane and tail.

'Her name is Ascot Park Astra; she is on the Australian junior team,' the girl informed me.

We chatted and then the Aussie duo picked up speed and galloped off into the distance.

It was out of sight out of mind. Until I got an unexpected phone call from the young Australian rider, Jenny. They wanted Ascot to stay in Dubai and were looking for someone to train her. She didn't have to ask twice!

Six months into her training Ascot, who we renamed Bisou, which means 'kiss' in French, was thriving. She had completed a couple of 120-km races and was ready for a 160-km race. I would have loved to own this horse, but I didn't. I don't like to have favourites but Bisou was special. Even Paris went all mushy around her.

'You're kidding me. You can't sell her!' I was on the phone to Jenny.

'We have no choice, we need the money,' Jenny explained.

I looked at Jeff. I knew they'd have no problem selling her, but to who? Bisou was a little fireball. She couldn't walk calmly anywhere, she only had fourth and fifth gears. In the wrong hands, she would be dead within the year. She was the kind of horse who would give you everything, even when she had nothing left. I was distraught and could do nothing.

But Jeff did.

It was coming up to Christmas, my favourite time of year. It was another early start. We strolled down the hill from the villa to the stables. Bisou was in the paddock standing waiting to be cuddled and kissed. It was her day off.

I looked and looked again!

'Why does she have a red ribbon on her?'

'She's a present for someone. Bisou is all yours!'

'What! You're joking? How?'

'Easy, they owed us money for training, we wanted the horse. We came to a deal. Simple.'

I was overwhelmed, truly dumbstruck. Bisou was all mine!

24
MUDDY CELEBRATIONS

Another addition to our race team came shortly afterwards, when we took the decision to compete on the European circuit during the summer months. Gaziza was a French-bred Barb Arab but looked more like a child's pony. She was small, grey and stocky. We had bought her from trainer Stephane Chazel in 2003. Gaziza was compact but a force to be reckoned with. In my first season riding her, we completed two 120-km races and finished a tough hilly 160-km race in Corsica. One of my most memorable early races with her was the 2003 European Championships in Ireland. The top six riders from each country were invited to compete.

'Can you believe this weather? It reminds me of Jerez last year,' commented Sandra, one of the team. We were cantering slowly at the back of the race, just taking our time.

She was right, it was chucking it down.

'Gaziza is a nightmare in the mud. If she thinks she's going to slip she comes to a grinding halt.'

Sandra laughed. She didn't realize how true my statement was.

When I arrived at the first vet check covered in mud, with branches and twigs coming out of my helmet, I knew I was in for one tough race. Gaziza had slipped down a small hill and lost all four legs. We hit the mud, both of us! This was not a good start.

Thankfully, by the 120-km stage the rain had stopped and Gaziza was back into overdrive. On the last but one loop, I raced alongside Sheikh Mohammed bin Rashid Al Maktoum, the Crown Prince of Dubai. We chatted for a while, but then I could sense he was eager to go faster and seemed to be concerned that I could outrace him.

'Sir, I am one loop behind you. So please go if you want?'

He nodded and laughed, and cantered off into the distance.

Gaziza was travelling well, but we were behind on time because of her mud phobia. As we were saddling her up for the last loop I could see a group of race officials coming towards us.

'Iona, sorry but we are here to advise you not to go out on the last loop. You will not make the minimum speed.'

I could not believe what they were saying. I had just completed 150 km and only had 10 km to go. I could feel the tears welling up.

Jeff stepped forward: 'No, she has the right to go out again. She will make up on the time.' He turned to me and gave me a big bear hug. 'Go get on your horse.'

The officials walked away muttering between themselves. At this stage of the race there were not many competitors left. All my teammates had either been vetted out or had retired, so it all rested on me. I looked over at Gaziza as she peacefully drank a massive amount of water from a large bucket and then she just turned and looked directly at me as if to say, 'I'm ready'.

But there was one remaining obstacle: it was pitch black and there were no beacons or illuminated signposts. I would be out there in the dark with no clue where to go. Being blonde and Irish, I'm no good with directions! But Larry, our chef d'equipe, had rallied the troops so that at every corner and every change of direction there would be an Irish team member with a fluorescent tube lighting the way.

Gaziza was champing at the bit and leaping around like a 2-year-old. I gave her a lose rein and she galloped out of the start gate, with cheers and screaming from the crowds. My cousins and friend showjumping trainer Jack Doyle had all come to support us. It all felt a bit surreal, even more so because Gaziza felt fresh and full of energy.

The next 10 km were almost heavenly. On every single corner and direction change I was cheered on with screams of excitement. Gaziza thundered on at a full out gallop to the point that we were now actually overtaking other riders. She hadn't gone this fast all day!

I felt tears of joy rolling down my cheeks, at one point it felt like my mum was travelling with me; her calming presence felt so real. Everything felt very dreamlike. With only a couple of kilometres to the finish, I saw Jeff on the side of the track jumping up and down, yelling, 'Wow! Go, go, Iona!'

He told me later he had phoned Stephane, Gaziza's trainer, and told him to get ready as I was nearly at the finish line. Stephane said that was impossible, Gaziza could not travel that fast. I could see the finish line and several riders in front of me. There was no slowing Gaziza, we overtook them all.

'Where on earth did you come from?' one of the riders shouted.

We crossed the finish line at a full out gallop, with screams and shouts of celebration. But finishing within the required speed does not automatically give you a placing, we still had to pass the vet inspection. If your horse is not fit to continue, then you're disqualified, even if you've completed the 160-km distance.

We also had to make sure that when we presented her to the vet, her heart rate was within the required range. If it was over 64 bpm we would be disqualified, but from day one of racing Gaziza she'd had an extraordinary heart rate, and today was no different. Even after the 10 km gallop, her heart rate was only 49 bpm. However, as the vets watched Gaziza trot, they all wanted to see her trot again. Not a good sign!

No way, I thought. She naturally had a weird movement from behind, partly because of the Barb in her.

I silently prayed to anyone who was listening.

The vets handed in their verdicts to the chief vet. He turned towards us.

'Congratulations, it's a pass.'

Not only had she been placed in the European Championships on home soil but Gaziza had travelled that last 10 km in 19.293 minutes, the third fastest of all the horses in the race. As you can imagine, the celebrations went on and on and on that night. It was worth the hangover the next day!

25
HOPE IN A DRAGON

Two months later I was on my way to an Arabian horse auction in Sharjah. A couple of friends, Jules and Jackie, were eager to go, so I thought I'd go along with them for the fun of it. As we walked in everyone was given a number just in case you wanted to bid.

'No, I won't need one,' I said as I handed it back to the lady.

She refused to take it back. 'You may need it.' I smiled and stuffed it in the pocket of my jeans.

I had no intention of buying any more horses, we had recently just added number twelve to the herd. He was a gift from a friend in Bahrain: a little jet-black pony who we called The Hobbit. Plus, we had just bought three youngsters from friend Stephane. So we really didn't need any more. Twelve was enough.

'Look at him, what a stunning stallion,' Jackie was drooling again.

'He *is* handsome and probably costs mega-bucks,' I agreed.

We were walking amongst the stables, checking out all the horses for sale.

'Wow she looks evil.' Jackie was right.

We all stopped and gawked at this beautiful liver chestnut mare with a facial expression that looked like something out of Jurassic Park. Her ears were pinned flat back and she repeatedly launched herself towards us in attack mode.

'Wow, lady, slow up! I think she's scared, not mean,' I sympathized. I truly believed that.

We carried on through the stables and out into the arena to take our seats. I kept wondering what had happened to that poor horse. Why was she so aggressive? Each Arabian horse came in to the arena with a professional handler. The horses trotted, cantered and pranced around on the end of a long leap rope, while the crowd clapped and cheered. Then they'd bid.

'Iona, look here comes that mare,' Jules was pointing towards the entrance.

She looked stunning. The handler was struggling to hold her, as she was leaping and dancing at the end of the rope. Actually, she looked more like a fire-breathing dragon. Even so, she was a magnificent animal.

To my surprise, people were bidding for her. *No one in their right mind would buy her,* I thought. I looked at Jules and Jackie and they stared back at me.

'Go on Iona, she's your type of horse?' whispered Jackie.

Suddenly my arm went up and I had put a bid in. Then a gentleman from Saudi upped the bid. I bid again. I kept thinking, *Jeff is seriously going to kill me!*

I was last to bid. It went silent. What now?

Then I felt a tap on the shoulder. 'Excuse me, sorry the bid wasn't high enough, so the horse is not sold.'

When Jeff returned home a couple of days later, he listened intently as I told him the story of the fire-eating dragon that we nearly bought. He laughed. A week later, I couldn't get her of my mind.

'Maybe you could go and have a look at her Jeff. Tell me what you think?'

Jeff went the following week. We had tracked her down to a well-known trainer and breeder.

'I put in a higher offer for her.'

I was shocked.

'Jeff, are you mad?'

'No, I know you liked her, and she is stunning. Unfortunately, the owner refused my offer.'

A month later there she was in our barn. The owner had changed his mind and had come back to us a couple of weeks later. Latifa was still grumpy but calmer. We had renamed her Latifa which in Arabic means 'hope'. We *hoped* she would change personality.

We now had a barn full of horses, every single one of them unique and slightly quirky. This quirkiness flowed over into our racing. Our seasons varied with the normal lows and highs, but we averaged about 70 per cent completion rate in our races. We had recently won a two-day 160-km race with our stallion Desert Dancer in Ireland. And Bisou had finished in 19th position in a 160-km night race in Abu Dhabi, which meant both were eligible for the next World Equestrian Games in Germany: if we were chosen.

With the operation growing, the next question was: are we in the right place? In my heart, I felt a change coming.

26
FRENCH CONNECTION

I could hear the mobile ringing, but where was it? Oops, under the hay net.

'Yes, yes, I can hear you.'

'Iona, good news, you and Bisou are on the team for the 2006 World Equestrian Games.' It was Kevin Crooke, one of the ILDRA officials.

'Awesome. Let's just hope I can get her ready in time.'

We had just relocated all thirteen horses to south-west France. Four years earlier, we had bought a property in the Gers region, just after the World Equestrian Games in 2002, and had spent the last couple of years renovating the house and building extensive equestrian facilities. It was horsey paradise. The constant travel between Dubai and France had become a struggle, especially with the horse training. Logistically, it wasn't working, so in the end it had been an easy decision.

Here I was in the beautiful French countryside wanting to settle in slowly, but no! After Kevin's surprise call, my priorities turned to Bisou and her next race. I was excited but concerned, as it normally takes a minimum of eight months to settle a horse into a new location and get them back into full training. I had five months to get her ready for the World Equestrian Games in Germany. This was just one of the challenges; the others were learning French, employing staff, finding a farmer to help look after the land and train thirteen horses. And not forgetting finding a vet, an accountant, a doctor, registering the business, and so on!

Nothing like a challenge!

I sat in the centre of Montreal Du Gers at one of the family-run cafés. This was our local village: quaint, beautiful and oozing personality. As the village was on the San Sebastian de Compostela pilgrimage route, it was a great place for people watching. Hikers and pilgrims came from across the globe. In amongst the hikers, I spotted a familiar face – it was Michel the deputy Mayor.

'Iona, just the person. I have some people you need to meet.' He gave me the normal three kisses and sat down. 'I will meet you here tomorrow, same time, and I'll take you to their chateau just outside Condom.'

I didn't really have a chance to say yes or no. He was up and gone in a flash.

We parked up outside this enormous equestrian arena. *Wow, this is incredible*, I thought. We had already passed acres and acres of vineyards and a gigantic, elegant chateau. I followed Michel into the stable area. Regal-looking stables were positioned around the most amazing indoor arena. It reminded me of the Spanish Riding School in Jerez. As I listened to the classical music being piped out into the arena, I thought I'd been transported to another planet.

I was introduced to Thierry and Silvia, the owners of Chateau de Gensac. They seemed like a lovely couple, but I wasn't sure why Michel had arranged this meeting. We chatted for twenty minutes and then it was obvious that our time was up. Thierry gave me his mobile number and we arranged to meet up the next time Jeff visited.

A couple of weeks later, Jeff and I were travelling down the long driveway towards the Gensac stables.

'Thierry said we only have thirty minutes.'

'Strange thing to say,' said Jeff.

'No, they're Swiss. That's normal. They seem to be very busy people and have a schedule. So, promise me you won't rabbit on when it's time to go.'

Jeff didn't answer. Four hours later, after having a tour of the stables, meeting all their beautiful horses and having lunch at their favourite pizzeria, we had all bonded. It was as if we had known Thierry and Silvia all our lives. With Jeff now working in Bahrain, Thierry and Silvia became a much-needed diversion from the training and racing. We all loved the same things: horses, dogs and cats, good food and wine. What else could you ask for? What really fascinated me about them was their total openness in talking about their Christian faith and how God seemed to be very much alive and active in their lives. We had some interesting discussions week after week while enjoying the Gascon culinary delights and Chateau Gensac's extraordinary wines.

'I think my view on Christianity is slightly warped, mainly because of my early school years,' I admitted, trying not to speak with my mouth full.

'You need to follow what's in the Bible and not get sidetracked by man-made religious rituals and traditions,' Thierry explained. 'The truth is in God's words, not man's.'

I talked briefly about my experience in Cyprus.

'I really felt like I had found a diamond in a field, but then I walked away! I felt the world was more real than God was.'

They lent me books and cassettes and I bombarded them with questions. They were patient. I was eager to know more. Thierry and Silvia had reignited something in me and I was curious to know more. Some nights I would lie awake just re-evaluating what they had said. In my heart, I believed God existed but not in the way Thierry and Silvia had mentioned. To them, God was a personal God who spoke to them, loved them and had a plan for them.

27
DOUBLE MUTTS

We were out at one of our first training rides with three young ladies who were now working for us. Leslie, Annabel and Ruth. We strolled single file down the narrow French country lanes and turned onto a forest track which would take us on a 10-km loop back to the farm. The horses were excited; it was their first time out, so they were all slightly skittish. With the World Equestrian Games looming, I didn't have the luxury of resting the horses. Bisou, as always, was in the front dancing from side to side, eager to go faster. I did my 'please slow down' whistle but she chose to ignore me.

Today everything felt good. Today it felt good to be alive. As we bounced along, I kept playing over the conversations I'd had with Thierry and Silvia the night before. I still found it odd that they prayed about everything. God guided every step they made. I also got to thinking about the racing and the time and the effort we were putting in to it. I loved what I was doing. I couldn't imagine not competing. It's what added value and meaning to my life. But I did have a question I couldn't answer. Why, after doing well in a race, like winning the 160-km race on Desert Dancer in Ireland, did I feel empty the next morning? I should have felt different, but no. I had so many unanswered questions, but if God really was who he said he was, then maybe I ought to take this a bit more seriously.

Before I knew it, we were back at the yard. I love to think and ride at the same time, it gives me clarity of thought. However, on this occasion, I ended up with more questions than clarity!

The weeks rolled into months and I embarked on a new daily routine. I read the Bible and talked to God for an hour a day, usually before breakfast. I'm not sure if you could call it praying, I just chatted away, believing that he was listening. Normally would start like this: 'If you're real God, you're going to have to help me here.' Some days I felt as if I was talking to someone, other days it was as if I'd turned into a mad woman and was just talking to myself.

After breakfast, the rest of the day was spent with the horses. By 7 p.m. I was exhausted. This is when I would curl up with a book or watch TV alongside Obelix, my loyal friend, guard dog and travel companion.

Obelix was just 2 years old and a giant of a dog. A dear friend, Emily, who raced on the French team had turned up at one of the international races with an unusual gift: a three-month-old Rottweiler-Beauceron cross puppy.

Emily handed me a giant brown fluff ball: 'You can't live alone in that farm house. So, we have a friend and companion for you.'

'Oh, how cute, but no! Jeff would divorce me. But thank you.'

I was still travelling between France and Dubai, so it was not feasible for me to have a dog, but Emily didn't give up. At the next race, Emily and the puppy reappeared. And suddenly common sense went out of the window. I had just successfully completed another 120-km race, so I was on a high and wasn't thinking straight when I agreed to take him.

That night we were all still in a hotel, as we were transporting the horses back home the following morning, so I made a bed up for Obelix in the bathroom. This was obviously wishful thinking, as within five minutes he was howling. The French are tolerant of dogs, but not one that keeps all their guests awake, so I had no option but to have him in bed with me.

As soon as he was next to me, he calmed down and went straight to sleep. The poor little thing was exhausted, and so was I. I had been up since 3:30 that morning and ridden 120 km in a very challenging race on Hyria, one of our most difficult horses, who had bolted with me on her in our last race. But just as I was nodding off, the fluffy bundle next to me started snoring loudly – and I mean loudly. I lay there wondering what I had let myself in for.

So most nights, when I wasn't with Thierry and Silvia, I would be cuddled up with Obelix, who now weighed in at 50 kilos and would eventually expand to a healthy 65 kilos. We had lost Beano in Dubai to cancer, at the age of 14. Having him put down broke my heart. We celebrated his life with chocolates, donuts and champagne, and when my friends left the villa, I lay on the ground where we had just buried him and sobbed until I could cry no more. In my heart, I cried silently for another five years.

It wasn't long before a second mutt joined the family. I had searched Europe high and low for an Italian greyhound puppy. I can't say I'm generally a fan of little dogs, but when I met my first Italian greyhound, it was love at first sight. We were staying at a wine chateau for the weekend with friends and I spotted this very elegant-looking dog curled up on a silk cushion in front of the fire. Within two days, we had formed a very special friendship. Then the hunt began. But one year later, we were still no closer to getting one.

'I think we have found one, Iona.' Renee who helped on the farm now and again had promised to carry on the search.

'Brilliant. I'll transfer the money and I'll pick him up when I get back next week.' I was in Bahrain with Jeff.

'Don't you want to see him first?'

'No, if we wait someone will nab him!'

Be Bop was unique and I could see why he hadn't been sold. His ears stuck up so much he looked a bit like a giant bat. But he was an Italian greyhound and I loved him. He accompanied me to the races and even slept in my bed. Spoilt! While Obelix, took on a new role of guarding the farm, Be Bop was my travel companion.

***

'Where's Be Bop?' I looked around and couldn't see him. Strange. He never left my side.

We were at a race in the north of France, a long way from home. I had been chatting to some of the riders when I realized Be Bop wasn't with me. I panicked.

'Have you seen my dog? Please, listen up. Has anybody seen my dog?'

'Excuse me but I think he ran when he saw those two big dogs,' the lady pointed at two German Shepherds.

Forty minutes had gone by and there was still no sign of him. Everybody joined in the search. We searched the stables, the forests, the barns. Nothing! I collapsed onto a bench and cried, *No way God, no way! Please help, please, please, please?*

I saw a car pull up and the official race photographer jumped out.

'Excuse me, I think I have your dog.'

I leapt up and ran towards the car. There, sitting in the passenger seat was Be Bop. He jumped into my arms and I burst into tears.

'Where did you find him?'

'About 5 km from here, running down the middle of the highway.'

When the photographer had left the venue to go back to his hotel, he was aware that there was a lost dog and when he saw Be Bop he had put two and two together.

'I pulled up and he just jumped into my car. It's a miracle he wasn't run over,' he explained.

Yes, it was truly a miracle! After that incident, Be Bop stayed on the lead.

28

FLYING BLUEBERRY

I was now one of the top five endurance riders in Ireland and had several horses who were competing at an international level, which meant more points in the World FEI rankings. I was competing every other weekend in and around Europe.

The 2006 World Equestrian Games in Agen came and went. Sadly, Bisou ran out of steam at the 120-km mark and was vetted out with a high heart rate. I knew that she hadn't had the right preparation and that helped with the disappointment. There would be many more races to come! I put it behind me and stepped back onto the rollercoaster, which took me on a new adventure most days.

On a regular working day at the yard, I'd spend a minimum of five hours in the saddle and then the rest of the day working the youngsters on the ground. I've learnt that horses are all unique and that there is no set pattern on how to train. But if you're willing to listen and watch, they educate you. And it's the difficult ones that really helped me. Like humans, horses come with baggage – some more than others. So, after buying a 'potential superstar', it can be months before you realize that somewhere along the line the horse you've purchased has been mistreated or has had a bad experience, and a roadblock appears in the training process.

One horse who changed my attitude to training was Blueberry, a little Arabian who was extremely well bred, and should have fast-tracked his way to the top in endurance. He arrived at our yards as a 2-year-old. He showed no signs of having issues until I started working on saddling him when he was 3 years old. I do desensitization exercises with all our horses by allowing them to experience different things in the round yard, which helps them overcome their fears. From the first day the saddle appeared, I realized Blue needed time, lots of time. Normally it would take a couple of days to get a horse comfortable with a saddle and bridle, but in Blue's case it took several months. I work under the philosophy that a horse is for life, so the groundwork must be done correctly, no matter how long it takes.

'Annabel, quick, open Blue's stable. Quick, Quick!' I screamed at the top of my voice.

I was in the round pen long-reining Blue, and as I moved behind him, he suddenly took off around the arena at a breakneck speed and subsequently crashed through the round yard gates and out into the main yard. It all happened so fast. I'd never seen a horse do this before! Normally, when a horse is scared, they tend to return to familiar surroundings, like their paddock or stable. Not Blue!

Blue circled the horse barn at a flat-out gallop then headed for the main farm gates.

'You have to be kidding me! Blue come back,' I screamed.

With the two long reins streaming behind him, he was now running blind. I could see he had lost all sense of reason: to him the reins were like two snakes chasing him. I watched as Blue disappeared into the distance towards the main road, leaving a cloud of dust behind him.

The first image that came into my head was a picture of Blue galloping head-on into an oncoming vehicle. This could be a catastrophe if he hit a motorist. I ran to the yard to get my mobile and called the local police station. The police arrived within 10 minutes of my call. They went off with the girls to search for him. I walked back to the house; my legs were like jelly. I just felt numb from head to toe. What could I do? I collapsed to my knees and prayed.

'Lord, help! Please help. You are the only one who knows where Blue is. You are the only one who can help.' I sobbed and sobbed. 'Lord, please help. You have the power to turn this situation around.'

Then my mobile started ringing. I braced myself for the worst.

'Madame Rossely, we've got your horse,' said the police officer.

'Is he okay? Is he injured? Were there any accidents?'

'No, but you need to come now and get him.'

I later found out that an elderly lady had just walked into the police station to say there was a horse tied up around a tree in the war memorial park in Castelnau D'Auzan, 7 km away from our farm. Blue had actually galloped down the middle of the main road for 7 km without coming into contact with any vehicles and he then managed to wrap himself around a tree with one of the long reins.

I hitched up the horse trailer, jumped in the Land Rover and sped out of the yard with Leslie and Ruth on board. As we drove down the main street of the village, we could see the park on the left-hand side. I pulled up and jumped out. I could not believe my eyes: there he was, grazing peacefully, not at all perturbed. He looked up as we approached, as if to say, 'It's you again!' and then went back to eating. We checked him over, and there was not a scratch on him except for the fact that his hoofs were hot and smelt like burning rubber. Shows how fast he was travelling.

Overnight, Blue became the talk off the town. On his rampage he had actually passed the local doctor's surgery, which was full at the time. The packed waiting room looked out onto the main road, and they all witnessed the spectacle of a little horse galloping at lightning speed into the village. Many of the locals said it was a miracle that he didn't come into contact with a car, truck or tractor on his 7-kilometre sprint.

Later that day I sat back in my office chair. A few hours earlier, I had been in the same room on my knees, crying and pleading for help. God had listened and helped. He really had! For months, I kept replaying in my mind over and over all the terrible things that could have happened. It was a miracle and an answer to prayer.

***

I began to realize that God and I were actually communicating, and that he was very active in my life. But he sometimes answered my prayers in a way I found difficult to comprehend.

I'd arrived at Thierry and Silvia's for lunch and a weekly catch-up. 'Sorry to hear about your accident Iona,' Silvia was looking at my bandaged hand.

'Yep it was just one of those freaky incidents. Teddy did a massive buck while we were out for a gallop. I landed on his neck and my finger snapped back and broke.'

I was due to race Jeff's horse Teddy that weekend, but not with a broken finger. He was strong as an ox and I needed at a minimum of ten fingers to hold him.

'Doctor's orders, no riding for three weeks . . . Maybe ten days,' I said smiling.

As Thierry placed the creamy truffle pasta dish in front of me, he said, 'Sometimes God steps in to guide us in a different direction. Maybe he wants you to spend more time with him.'

Prior to this accident, I had been asking God to show me how I could get to know him better. This was not what I'd had in mind!

Six months later, I was sitting in our accountant's office going through the wages and tax forms. 'That finger looks like it's broken, it's blue.'

'Hmm, maybe, not sure,' I replied, wanting to concentrate on the work at hand.

'Iona, I would pass by the doctor's surgery and get it checked out.'

'Maybe.'

A couple of days earlier, I had been training Obelix. We had recently installed an invisible fence system around the garden area. I had him on a long horse lead which was wrapped around my hand. I was talking to a friend when Obelix spotted a friend's puppy coming towards us. Forgetting about the electric fence, he leapt forward and immediately got electrocuted and bolted. Unfortunately, the rope unravelled but stayed wrapped around my little finger which snapped backwards, breaking both the bone and tendon. So here I was, trying to pretend that, if I ignored it, the injury would disappear. This time I was off for a good six weeks.

Was God trying to get my attention, I wondered? It seemed as though every time I truly opened up and cried out for help, I would get injured. Maybe it was just a coincidence, but just to cover all bases, I would request a no-injury, hospital-free answer to prayer when possible. Sometimes it worked!

29
COMMUNITY CHALLENGE

I loved my talks and debates with Thierry and Silvia, but I felt isolated. I wanted to be more involved in a wider community. So I toddled off to the local Anglican church in Condom.

I went to the church a couple of times, but the traditional service and rituals were very different from what I was experiencing in my walk with God. It was very formal and structured; I needed something more personal and informal. But I did find a community. It just happened to be in another country!

Jeff was now working in London overseeing the refurbishment of the Four Seasons Hotel on Park Lane. Part of his work contract included a beautiful rented apartment in Kensington. I enjoyed bouncing between the country life in France and the busy city life of London.

Jeff and I were sitting in a French restaurant on Brompton Road, watching streams of young people stroll across the road. It was Sunday evening and they were heading to Holy Trinity Church. I was stuffing my face with garlic mushrooms and sipping red wine.

'That must be a popular church. It's unusual to see so many young people,' Jeff observed.

Jeff was right. I'd heard of Holy Trinity Brompton, but I was taken aback by the number of people flowing towards the entrance.

'Remember I did the Alpha Course with Thierry and Silvia? That's where it originated.' The previous year I had done a six-week Alpha course with Thierry and Silvia. I absolutely loved it. Why? Because it didn't ram religion down your throat, it opened doors, it allowed me to ask questions, and it allowed me to disagree without being judged. At the end of it, I was blown away by what I'd learnt. The course gave me a complete picture of why we were on planet earth.

'Do you fancy coming to church with me one Sunday?'

Jeff looked up from his game pie and stared blankly at me.

'Maybe, but not to one that's overly lively.'

The next day I was on the internet and found a sister church to Holy Trinity, St Paul's, which was located within a fifteen-minute walk of our apartment. The people were great, the service was personable and informal. It was relaxing and comfortable and felt like a church should feel – welcoming and loving. The first time Jeff and I went, halfway through the service I became tearful. I felt overcome by a sense of love. Jeff glanced over at me with a 'What's wrong now?' expression. And I glared back with a 'Stop looking at me like that!' stare.

My time in London was limited because of my racing commitments. But when I was there, St Paul's was always part of my agenda, plus Holy Trinity Brompton's bookshop and café. Mixing the French countryside with the hustle and bustle of London was a real blessing.

***

In the last twelve months, I had competed throughout France in most of the major FEI rides. I had managed to qualify for all the big competitions and finish with some good placings. One of them was with my French pony Gaziza, who had completed a 160-km race in St Galmier, which qualified her for the next European Championships in Portugal. I was disappointed that I was the only Irish rider to qualify, but was even more disappointed when I found my entry had not been formally submitted to the FEI.

'No way! What do you mean?' I shouted down the phone. 'That's two years of training wasted because someone forgot to enter me. Tell me this is a prank?' I wasn't a happy bunny! I was standing next to Thierry and Silvia, overlooking their lush green horse paddocks. They were looking slightly shocked by my yelling, but I didn't care.

'Yes, try again. I'm not accepting this. You need to speak to the FEI!' I hung up. I was seething! When you put every waking hour into getting a horse ready for a particular race, then yes, I felt I had a right to be upset. Sadly, even with ILDRA trying their best to resurrect the situation, the FEI would not accept a late entry.

As Gaziza was race fit and ready to go, I entered her into a two-day, 160-km two-star race at Labenque in France. I was still devastated not to be competing in the Europeans, but this was the next most prestigious race on the calendar, with 129 riders from twelve nations.

I stood looking at Gaziza in her stable. She had just completed 80 km and had finished in the top twenty on the first day.

'Do you think she can keep up that pace tomorrow?' asked Stephane. He looked concerned. Gaziza was travelling at just under 19 km/h. It was the fastest she'd ever gone over 80 km.

'I'm not sure. But she felt strong. I was struggling to hold her, so I let her go.'

I've learnt not to get too excited on the first day at two-day rides because of the vet check the following morning. Many horses are vetted out even before the start.

'Excuse me, please can you move away from the start line,' I shouted. I was on Gaziza, who was throwing an absolute wobbly over an injured man with crutches. For some unknown reason she had always had a phobia about crutches; it was almost as if she was seeing a twenty-foot dinosaur on the verge of attacking her. She had successfully passed the vetting for the second day and was now at the start line prancing from side to side like a fire-breathing dragon, ready for war.

'Rossely, go, go!'

As soon as my name was called we were off, not at a canter but a flat-out gallop.

Blimey, I think someone has given my little horse a brain transplant! This is not normal behaviour, I thought. She flew around the course, overtaking riders whenever possible. Gaziza recorded a time of 20 km/h on her first loop. She was getting faster, not slower. After the vet check and mandatory rest period, Gaziza was waiting on the start line for the last 40 km and the final run home.

'Excuse me miss, can you tell me what you feed your horse?' one of the riders asked. Gaziza was now rearing. She never rears! Ever! Everyone was watching her. It was as if she was possessed. She practically flew around the last 40 km, it was like sitting on a winged horse. Normally the last loop of any race is a little stressful, but not this one – it was a breeze.

Stephane, Gaziza's original owner and trainer came up and gave me a big hug. 'I cannot believe that result. Congratulations! I'd never have guessed Gaziza could go that fast.' He patted me on the back. 'Well done to you both.'

We were placed in fifteenth position with an average speed of 18.1 km/h. The bitterness and disappointment of the Europeans had diminished. Now on to the next goal!

30
MIRACLE HORSE

Bisou's warm muzzle was pressed against my back as I was sorting out her night-time hay. She was trying to give me a massage but sometimes got over eager and would nibble. Painful!

'Oh! Careful young lady, that's my skin!' I turned around and gave her a big hug.

'Hope you're ready for this big race?' She looked at me as if to say, 'Ready and willing.'

It was hard to believe that three years earlier we almost lost her to a rare disease. I had been competing in the 160-km Florac Race, renowned as the toughest race in Europe, on her stable mate Gaziza, when I had received a call from our vet in Dubai saying that Bisou had been rushed in to the Dubai Equine Hospital. After a few frantic calls, we were told that she had been diagnosed with Nile River Fever, the first recorded case to affect a horse in Dubai.

'Iona we are sorry, but her chances of surviving are very slim.' Dr Jannette was one of the best, and I knew she was in good hands.

'There must be a way of saving her,' I implored.

But Jannette warned me again to prepare myself for the worst. 'Not many horses survive Nile River Fever. It attacks their nervous system and immune system. I am sorry Iona.'

I just felt numb! For days I could not speak, I just wallowed around in a dark place. But I did pray. I prayed every minute of the day. However, each day I would get an update and each day it seemed like she was deteriorating. When she collapsed and was unable to get up, the vet called to say they may have to put her down.

'Please, just give her one more day,' I pleaded. I got off the phone and posted on my social media sites asking every person I knew to start praying for a miracle. I knew God could help. And the more people who prayed, the better. I wasn't going to give up on her.

I was sitting in the car outside an antique shop; Jeff was inside browsing. I was still in shut-down mode and unable to face the outside world, especially a French antique shop. My mobile started ringing and as I saw the number my heart broke. *Please God, no!*

'Iona she's up, she stood up! And listen . . .'

I was not sure what I was listening to. It sounded like a munching sound.

Dr Jannette was back on the phone: 'She just suddenly stood up and started eating her hay. Iona this is unbelievable!'

The vets were totally dumbfounded; I think they were as elated as I was. I could not stop crying. Tears of joy streamed down my face as I bolted out of the car and into the antique shop. The expression on Jeff's face was one of horror as I burst through the double doors at full speed screaming, 'She's okay, she's okay, she's going to be okay!'

I stood now looking at her in her stable. It was still hard to believe that she had survived, but I also remembered a promise I had made: *God if you heal her and restore her to full health, I will never race her again.* I'm sure he's used to humans breaking their promises, but in the pit of my stomach, I felt bad – really bad.

And now I had her lined up for the 2010 World Equestrian Games in Kentucky, USA. But she still had one small hurdle to jump. To qualify for WEG, I needed to complete a 160-km international race.

Leading up to this race, Bisou had already completed two 120-km races in France; now she just needed to complete a 160-km race within the allotted time. I had chosen a race in Portugal. Easy, I thought.

Little did I know that this trip would change my life, turning it upside down and inside out.

31
SAVING GRACE

We pulled up at the race venue. It had taken us two days, with a couple of overnight stops. Ruth and her sister Jane unloaded Bisou; it looked like we were the first competitors to arrive. I wanted Bisou to get a good rest and settle before the race in two days. Bisou strolled out of the box looking fresh and calm. Her big brown eyes surveyed her new surroundings. She was such a stunning-looking mare.

Bisou, the girls and I had a day to chill out before the training ride. On day two the venue was slowly filling up with horses, crews and riders. I stood overlooking the lush fields that disappeared out towards the ocean. I'd chosen this race because the terrain was sandy and flat: ideal conditions for Bisou. She liked to travel at a fast pace, so this was ideal. My aim was simple: I just needed to complete the 160 km to qualify.

'Ruth, I will be back in a couple of hours,' I said as I mounted Bisou.

'No worries, we'll be here. We will clean up her stable and start race preparations for tomorrow.'

I headed out towards one of the marked endurance tracks. Bisou, as always, was very excitable and bouncing around eager to start trotting.

'We are walking young lady. You need to stretch out your muscles,' I told her.

She had her deaf ears on as normal! After thirty minutes, I took her into a slow trot. But within a minute I realized that there was something very wrong. I could feel her cramping up. She was trying to move forward, but nothing was happening. I could see she was sweating, and white foam had appeared on her neck. I leapt off her. I pulled out my mobile.

'Ruth, we have a problem. Bisou is tying up. I will walk her back slowly, but you need to find a vet. Please be quick.'

I knew instantly what was happening. My first endurance horse, Aktash, had suffered with this a couple of times. Tying up is when the horse's muscles go into spasmodic cramping. It is usually caused by a change of food or stress.

'Where's the vet?' I asked as soon as we got back.

Ruth looked even more stressed than me. 'No one knows. There are no race officials here yet.'

We unsaddled Bisou, who was now shaking and sweating all over. I knew she needed liquids and that this had to be done intravenously as soon as possible. Waiting could cause liver, kidney and muscle damage. When the vet arrived three hours later, I was on the verge of having an emotional meltdown. Bisou's whole metabolic system had gone into shutdown.

'It looks like a chronic tying up. I will start her on fluids.'

I glared at the FEI vet. 'It's only chronic because you should have been on site three hours ago,' I was seething. 'She also had Nile River Fever three years ago, but her immune system recovered.'

The vet nodded and went back to inserting a needle into Bisou's neck. As I stood and watched the veterinary team work on her, it was like a bad dream. *This cannot be happening!* I thought. It was critical to get fluids into her as fast as possible to stop her system from shutting down any further. While every man and his dog were now in Bisou's stable trying to help, I was on the phone bawling my eyes out to Silvia.

'Why has God just abandoned me? How could he let this happen?' I was angry and upset. Really angry. 'What was he thinking, allowing this to happen to me?'

Silvia just listened and remained silent.

'I feel like he's up and left me. I don't understand.'

'Iona we are here for you. Call me tomorrow and let me know how she is.'

No answers to my questions.

Jeff was calling back.

'Sorry I was in a meeting. All okay?'

I ranted and raved for ten minutes.

'Iona, there are many more races. And Bisou will recover.'

'Yes, I know, but this was my last chance to qualify for the World Equestrian Games.'

'It's just a race!'

Not what I wanted to hear. It was more than just a race. I'd failed. This would be the first time I hadn't qualified for one of the World events. And one of my best horses would probably never race again.

Several hours later, Bisou was on the road to recovery. It was midnight. We drove back to our hotel. As I walked into my room, I totally lost it! I picked up my suitcase and anything else that wasn't bolted to the floor and threw it around the room. I screamed and cried. I felt helpless, angry and broken. It was as though someone had just sawn me in half. *Why God, why? I thought we had a partnership!*

The next morning, I felt no better, and I appeared in the breakfast room with large dark circles under my eyes and a look that told most onlookers to stay away from me. We stayed on at the race venue for another couple of days to give Bisou time to recover before the long journey home. Two days of driving became two days of thinking: I kept replaying over and over in my mind what I could have done differently, but I had no answer. I felt gutted and empty. It was a relief to pull into the stable yard. To my surprise, I saw Thierry and Silvia, plus one other person walking towards me.

'We thought you might like some company, and we've bought dinner and lots of wine,' Thierry smiled and gave me a hug. Silvia took hold of my arm and squeezed it as if to say, 'Stay strong we're here for you!' They introduced me to Peter, a church elder from Zurich, who staying with them.

The fire was lit, and we sat relaxed and content after an awesome beef casserole and a couple of glasses of their Gensac wine. I relived the last seven days and how I felt. Thierry and Peter suggested we pray together for clarity and wisdom on the way forward. They prayed. I couldn't. I was angry with God and deeply hurt. I sat there with my arms folded, unable to participate. I just didn't have the willpower and I was hurting too much. I was not in the mood to talk with God! Peter seemed like a nice guy, but by the end of the evening was asking me very strange questions about my relationship with Jesus, such as whether I had surrendered total control of my life to him. I had no idea what he was getting at.

That night I lay awake trying to figure out why I felt so broken. Racing had become my life. Actually, it was more than that, it was my identity. From an early age, my personal identity and who I was had come from competing. Being successful in sport gave me a sense of acceptance and value. I was fanatical about making sure I was a 'somebody', that's why I gave 100 per cent in everything I did. It's all or nothing, that's my personality. I would never do a sport that I wasn't good at, as I hate to fail, it's just not in my DNA. But here I was, a failure!

The next morning, I woke up feeling the same – depressed. I was worn out and miserable. It was as if something inside me had died. I walked down the stairs into the kitchen in a blanket of self-pity. I spotted my Bible and notebook on the table. I couldn't think, I just stared at the book.

Suddenly, an overwhelming sense of love flooded into the kitchen. I stood rigid. An engulfing and overpowering presence surrounded me. I could not move. I dropped to my knees and cried. I couldn't stop. At that precise moment, I knew Jesus had not abandoned me – I had abandoned him! I felt his arms around me, and an overwhelming sense of love – an indescribable love.

My mind surged into flashbacks, memories of the last two years. I could see that at every step of my journey, at every major decision I took, it was me who led the way. God was with me, but I was calling the shots. It was time to let go and let Jesus take the reins.

I sat at the kitchen table and cried. But my tears were tears of joy, not sadness. I felt changed from the inside out. I felt different. It was as if a great weight had been lifted from my shoulders. I felt a freedom that I'd never felt before. It was freedom that allowed me to be me, it was a freedom not to try and be somebody I wasn't.

In the twinkling of an eye, my life turned upside down.

32
LOSING YOUR MARBLES

It was evening hay time! I strolled over to the barn. We were now up to nineteen horses, every one of them unique and loved.

'Good evening girls and boys.'

Every head popped over the stable door. Charlie, the clown of the family, was throwing his head up and down as if he was in a rock concert. Latifa was gnashing her teeth and Paris was impatiently kicking his door. As I threw the hay over, I did a quick check of each horse. Thankfully, none of them had spotted the carrot I had in my back pocket.

Bisou waited patiently. I slid open her door and stepped in. She went straight to my pocket. Hoping her neighbours wouldn't spot the treat, I quickly gave her the carrot. She had recovered well from her ordeal, but I knew she would never be able to race again.

'You know Bisou, we both have to be thankful. You're going to have a permanent holiday and my life will also be very different. In a good way!' Bisou dropped her head and nudged me for more treats. I turned off the lights and closed the large barn doors. What a day!

I knew my life would change after my encounter that morning and I'd already decided on one change. Now I just had to break the news to Jeff.

I picked up my mobile, thinking, *Lord you're going to have to help me here. I'm not sure how Jeff will react to this.*

'Jeff, I've decided to do a two-year online theology course. It's a long story of how I got to this decision, but I know it's the right move.' It went very quiet on the other end of the phone. Silence. *Had he fallen off his chair or worse, had he had a stroke?*

'Hello! Is anybody there?'

Jeff was back working in Bahrain.

'A couple of days ago you were deeply depressed and today you're wanting to study theology. It doesn't make sense!'

'You'll understand when I explain. Probably best in person, though, not on the phone.'

The next phone call was to Silvia.

I could hear their car pull up and strolled to the front door. Thierry and Silvia always came bearing gifts, normally in the form of red wine. We kissed and hugged, and I launched into my Jesus experience. They looked rather shocked. I could see they were concerned that I had imagined it all. So, I played it down a bit and then they relaxed.

I'd cooked chicken paprika with brown rice, a recipe that you could rarely mess up. I wanted desperately to explain how I felt, but as they were fairly conservative in their views, I didn't want them to think I'd turned into a raving lunatic.

'I realized a couple of days ago that I had it all wrong. My relationship with God was a bit one-sided. It was all about me and what I wanted.' I poured wine into our glasses.

'So, I've made a radical decision: I'm letting go and letting God take the reins.'

'So now what?' Thierry was intrigued.

'Bible college.'

'Wow, that's a big step. Are you sure?' said Silvia.

'What about the racing?' She looked concerned.

'Not sure,' I said.

I really didn't know how to balance the racing and my competitive nature with what God wanted. I also knew that Jeff was concerned, as he knew I could be compulsive and obsessive. With nineteen horses, five staff and a rigorous training and racing schedule lined up for the year ahead, it was going to be an interesting time.

God, what do I do? I knew inside that I had changed. I no longer had the passion to spend five to seven hours a day on horseback or compete in a 120- or 160-km race. I loved the horses and was still competitive, but my priorities had shifted.

***

I applied to the Master's College and was accepted. I know I'm not an academic, I'm more a sporty, outdoor person, but I loved the learning. I sat at my desk, surrounded by all my new study books. *This is really not me!* I chuckled to myself. But here I was embarking on a theology course. I had also radically changed my daily routine: I worked the horses from nine to three and then I retreated to my office to study for three hours or more. Plus, I had reduced my racing by 50 per cent.

'What are you studying, Iona?' Ruth had just dropped by to say goodbye before she left for the day.

'Good question!' I laughed and spun around a few times on my swivel chair.

'It's a course in biblical studies.'

Ruth looked no wiser!

'I want to learn more about God and who he is. The more we know about God, the more we experience him.'

'How's that relevant to anything?' Ruth was known for her cheeky attitude.

'Well I believe that there is so much more to life, so I'm searching for answers to questions.'

Ruth smiled and pulled her rucksack over her shoulder. 'When you find the meaning of life let me know.' As she walked away, Ruth yelled, 'You need to watch *Hitch Hiker's Guide to the Galaxy*. They've already found the answer – it's number 42.'

'Funny, ha ha!' I yelled back.

With the racing schedule not being so hectic, Jeff and I agreed it was also time for a vacation.

***

I peered out of the small window as we soared over the green fields of England. We were on our way to New York for a week and then stopping over to see my father. He had relocated to the USA from Cyprus after marrying American-born Kathleen. I giggled remembering how they first met.

'I'm coming to stay for Christmas, Iona,' he had informed me.

'That's great news, Daddy. Is Veronica coming with you?'

'No, I have a new lady in my life.'

He then went on to explain that he hadn't actually met her yet, but they had been corresponding on the internet. Now I was worried that my father had lost all his marbles. This did not sound like him.

'Kathleen will arrive a week before we fly to you.'

'So that's single beds then Daddy?'

'I'll let you know,' he laughed and said goodbye.

Whenever Jeff and I had visited my father in Cyprus before we were married, we were always allocated single beds. So, I was just reminding him how things worked in our family. The week before they were due to fly over, I got a text message saying 'It's one bed and it's a good one!'

Now I was really worried!

I was even more convinced he had problems when, on the first evening together, as we all sat down with a glass of champagne, he suddenly jumped up and said he had an announcement.

'We're getting engaged!'

Silence.

It was as if I'd just been hit by a freight train. I couldn't speak. I was stunned. Kathleen was a lovely lady. Actually, she looked very much like my mother. But I wasn't expecting this. They had been together less than ten days. I looked at Jeff in disbelief.

'Congratulations to you both!' said Jeff.

I wasn't sure how I felt. I was worried for my dad. This wasn't his normal behaviour. We were all still mourning the loss of my mum; it had now been ten months since her passing. I know my parents hadn't been together since I was 11 years old, but this seemed like the wrong time. This was the first Christmas without my mum and we were now supposed to celebrate my father's engagement. It didn't sit well with me!

Over the next couple of days, my attitude did change. It had been a long time since I'd seen my father so happy. He was totally lovestruck. Kathleen seemed to be kind, compassionate and was very genuine in her affections. Daddy was eager to explain that he had never entertained or even thought about internet dating. He claimed that he saw a site called *Match.com* and thought it was a football results site. I'm not sure I totally believed him.

It was a whirlwind romance from start to finish and within a year, they were married. Another two years later, they had relocated to Aiken in South Carolina.

So here we were, on our way to visit them for the first time. I was looking forward to the break. The horses were on their annual rest, and with two semesters of study finished and put to bed, I was ready for a holiday.

It was also a vacation that triggered an unpredicted move!

33
A PUNCTURED INTESTINE

New York was awesome, but after a couple of days of sightseeing, I was becoming increasingly concerned about not been able to get through to the girls on the farm, on either mobile or land line.

'Jeff there has to be a problem. We cannot even get hold of Thierry or Silvia.' We were sitting in Starbucks, next to the Empire State Building.

'I wonder if it's got anything to do with the hurricane that was heading towards Spain?' he said, as he flicked through the newspaper.

'I doubt it. It looked like it was going in the other direction.' I sipped my extra-hot latte and prayed silently. I was finding it difficult to enjoy anything. I was worried.

I nearly dropped my latte when my mobile started ringing. My ringtone at the time 'Oh Happy Day' was probably not the most appropriate for this particular day. It was Ruth. The connection was muffled and crackled badly.

'I can hardly hear you. Is everything okay?'

'We got hit by the hurricane. Everyone is alright, but we have no power. Could be another week or more before we get it back.'

'What about the horses?'

'They are okay. Shaken but no injuries. But the big oak tree came crashing down and missed the house by only a couple of feet.'

We found out later than the hurricane had suddenly changed course unexpectedly. Most of the roads were blocked, and many of our trees were now no longer. Our whole area had been flattened. There had been winds of up to 200 km/h, 1.7 million homes without power and 27 fatalities.

Even though it was not good news, it was a relief to know they were all okay. Later that day, Ruth called to say that Thierry had battled through the fallen trees to get to our farm to check all was okay. That's what you call friendship!

Now I could relax and chill with the family. The town of Aiken was quirky and full of character. I had thought my dad was exaggerating when he said that there are horses everywhere. He wasn't. Aiken is the horse capital of the region. I felt very much at home. I was, however, rather taken aback by how involved my father and Kathleen were in community life. From helping at the soup kitchen to fundraising, and they were passionate about church life. That was something we didn't have in France. I could feel a restlessness well up inside me.

'Jeff, have you ever considered that France may not be the right place to retire?'

We were on our way back to France after two wonderful weeks in Aiken.

'Not really, but you're obviously having second thoughts.'

'I would like to be more involved in the community we live in. I just don't see that happening in France.' I was on a roll now. 'Plus, you don't speak French.' He laughed.

'And you do?'

'Yes, I'm fluent after a bottle of red.'

I had planted seeds. Now it was best to stay quiet on the subject. I silently spoke to God instead: *Lord if this is a good idea, please guide us to where we should go.*

A month later, Jeff and I were scrolling through the internet looking at farms in the UK. Jeff had agreed that an English-speaking community may be better for us long term. Jeff returned to Bahrain and I balanced my days with studying, playing with the horses and finding a new home for us on the web. I was also due to visit Bahrain in a couple of weeks, so I was eager to get organized so that I could give Jeff recommendations on potential farms.

Five days before my trip to the Middle East, I woke feeling a bit weird. It felt as though I had a severe case of haemorrhoids. I drove to the local pharmacy. Being slightly embarrassed, I explained in broken French that my husband had haemorrhoids and needed treatment. I'm not a very good liar and they looked at me with this 'we know your husband is away' type of look. Anyway, the cream did nothing for the pain. So, I went to the local doctor, who gave me more cream. Which also did nothing!

'Jeff I'm not sure what to do. I can hardly move. There is no way I can get on that plane.'

'You need to call the doctor again,' he advised.

'I'll wait and see how I am in the morning.' Overnight my condition worsened dramatically. I now had a very high temperature and the pain was unbearable. I put an emergency call in to the doctor and he rang through to the hospital to get me admitted immediately. Ruth drove me to Bordeaux emergency department. By this stage, I was unable to stand, and after a quick examination I was rushed into the operating theatre.

'You are one very lucky lady. We found approximately five litres of pus inside you. Another couple of hours and you would have been a goner!' the surgeon told me.

'I don't understand. How did I get an infection?'

The surgeon explained that it would have been triggered by either a fish or chicken bone puncturing through my intestine. In medical terminology, they call it a fistula.

'You're going to be out of action for at least three months.' He smiled and walked away, then stopped and turned as he got to the door. 'You should be thankful. That was a close call.'

I was now housebound. Every second day, a community nurse came to change my dressing, which taught me serious lessons in humility. Not pleasant! I later found out that my doctor had absconded the day he admitted me to hospital. Yep, he had just packed his bags, left his wife and business and taken off with a younger woman. He'd obviously had other things on his mind when he originally misdiagnosed my condition.

I lay on the sun lounger in the back garden. It was another sunny day, the birds were singing, I could see Blue, Simmy and Charlie playing tag in their field below, and I felt rested and peaceful. I'd had many talks with God about my illness, including the normal 'Why this is happening?' questions. I didn't get an answer. But what I did know was that this recovery time was allowing me to connect with him on a much deeper level. It was good to step out of the daily routine and take a reality check on what was important.

It also gave me time to check out farms. I thought Devon seemed to be the ideal place for us. Why not? All the tourists go there, so it must be good. At this stage, I was unaware that it was one of the wettest places in England. I found several potential farms and Jeff agreed to go and check them out. As I was unable to travel because of my medical condition, I waited patiently for his thoughts.

'There is only one I like. It's the one on the bottom of your list.'

'That would be about right,' I said. When it comes to buildings and restoration projects Jeff sees things no one else can, so I remained optimistic.

'It's just outside the Dartmoor National Park. The village has two pubs, a church and, especially for you, a doctor's surgery right next to the farm.' It was a standing joke that wherever we lived it needed to be near a medical centre.

'Very funny. After this illness I'm trying to stay clear of doctors.' Two months later, I was on my way to check out our new farm.

One of my favourite things about England is the pubs. And here we were sitting in Cheriton Bishop, Devon after visiting our next home, in one of the two pubs in the village. Jeff was busy drawing up plans for our stable extension on a serviette and I sipped my gin and tonic.

I tugged at Jeff's sleeve whispering, 'I know that this might sound weird, but the gentleman behind me sounds familiar. He also knows a great deal about endurance.'

Jeff peered over my shoulder. I didn't want to appear rude and turn, so I waited.

'I think you should turn and say hello,' Jeff was smiling.

I could not believe my eyes. It was Hugh, the official British Endurance Team vet.

'What are you doing here?' I asked.

'I live here, this is my local pub. More to the point, what are you doing here? I thought you lived in France.'

'Yes, sort off, but we've also just bought Coxland Farm.'

'Wow, that's awesome! We'll be neighbours, and you've got the best vet at your service.'

Hugh had helped me out at a number of races with some of our horses, most notably, at the Europeans in France when Hyria needed emergency fluids. Not sure where the Irish team vet was, but Hugh had stepped in and saved the day.

I had begun to see that once you connect with God, there is no such thing as a coincidence. I took this as another confirmation that this was the right place and a good move. The other confirmation was that even though there was a property recession, our French farm, Bastian, looked like it was going to sell sooner than we thought.

For me it was a short visit, but Jeff stayed on to start the renovation works while I flew back to Toulouse. Shifting nineteen horses, five cats and two dogs would need a lot of pre-planning and organization.

Over a five-year period, we had increased in numbers, not only with the horses and dogs, but also with the cats. We arrived from Dubai with two cats, Spit, the wild one and a stable cat, Minnie. We were now leaving France with three extra moggies: Harry Potter and Asterix, who we rescued as kittens, and Bubbles who was made homeless when her owners divorced.

It was time to work out how to transport our 'zoo' to the United Kingdom.

34
SHEEP ATTACK

It took Jeff just a year to oversee the renovations on our new abode. He was now officially retired, so it gave him a much-needed project to keep him mentally stimulated. And what a project! Coxland was a Grade 2 listed building. The main structure was originally an old school house, with another house linked by an orangery with glass panels that opened up to the sky. It was built in 1536, when Henry VIII was on the English throne. It oozed character: fireplaces, wooden floors, timber beams and three-foot-thick cob walls. On the equestrian side, we had 23 stables, a round pen, dressage arena and a mega-size horse walker, plus 50 acres of land. It was our dream property.

Twelve months flew by, and in October 2010, I arrived with the zoo in tow. Two weeks later, so did the snow, which sent us into total chaos. The water pipes froze, pipes exploded, and we were unable to get the horses out of their stables. They were literally snowed in! Thankfully, a group of villagers came to the rescue with shovels and spades to help dig them out. This was truly what you call 'community spirit'.

With the horses, dogs and cats settled in and new staff on board, the next task for me was finding a church community. The church bells were ringing as we strolled down our lane towards the local church. St Mary's had been built in the 13th century and stood strong and elegant amongst the thatched cottages and rose-covered gardens.

'Iona, don't get your hopes up. This may not be the right church for us,' warned Jeff.

'Of course, it will be, silly. It's right on our doorstep,' I laughed.

We stepped in through the arched doors. There weren't many people. No one turned to look. No one said hello. *Hmm, not very friendly*, I thought. One hour later, I sat looking at my hands and playing with my wedding ring, feeling a bit down. This was probably not the right place for us. Jeff led the way out. I saw the minister shaking hands with people as they left. He shook our hands and just looked at us. No welcome, no chitchat. Nothing! We walked home in silence. We let the dogs out and checked on the horses.

'After that, I think I need a drink. Let's walk to the pub?' suggested Jeff.

'Sounds like a plan,' I agreed.

As we walked into the pub, we recognized several of our friends and settled into a Sunday afternoon chill-out. We had a community in the pub! As Jeff had, over the last twelve months, got to know nearly everyone in the village, it was easy to fit in with the locals. Couldn't say the same for the church. But I wasn't prepared to give up just yet!

By the fifth visit, it was obvious that this was not the church for us. But on our last visit to St Mary's, we did acquire two new friends, Sandra and Chris, who lived just at the bottom of one of our paddocks. As the service came to an end, I knew in my heart we were barking up the wrong tree. I gathered my things and then heard a very posh voice say, 'I bet you won't come back after that.' We all laughed. Sandra introduced herself and her husband Chris. Together we walked up the road chatting and laughing. It was the start of many fun get-togethers.

***

Be Bop was sitting on my lap trying to lick my ears, which I hate. At the same time, I was having a talk with God. *We have a great community but no church. We need to find one. Help!* It wasn't long before we had an answer . . .

Out on one of our country walks, and following a new hiking trail through farmland, we must have taken a wrong turn somewhere.

I turned and yelled at Jeff, 'Quick run, they're chasing us, quick, run!'

Jeff couldn't stop laughing: 'Iona they are sheep, not bulls.'

'But there's so many. We'll get crushed! There must have been more than a hundred sheep galloping towards us. I ran.

Now we were safely back on a lane heading home.

'Hello, hello! Are you guys lost?'

'Not any more, but we did take a detour, into a sheep paddock.'

He stood with arms on hips and gave a broad smile,

'Yes, they're my sheep. Very friendly. Love people. Love cuddles.' Farmer Ian introduced himself and explained that some of the sheep had been bottle-fed as lambs, so they associated people with food.

'You must be the new owners of Coxland Farm? Please come and join us for afternoon tea.' Three hours later, we ventured home in the dark.

'What a lovely family,' said Jeff.

'Yes, and it looks like we may have found the right church.'

Ian and his wife Sarah had invited us to their church in Crediton, which was about a twenty-five-minute drive from the farm. Just by listening to how they described it, I had no doubt this would be the one for us.

'Welcome, welcome.' We were greeted at the door by a very jolly couple. As they handed us an information sheet, the young lady said, 'Please come in, help yourself to tea or coffee and sit anywhere you like.'

This is more us, I thought. Within a minute of stepping through the door, we were bombarded by people saying hello and asking us who we were. Finding the right church community was important – even more so for Jeff than for me. He still wasn't convinced by the 'Christian' way of life, but was willing to accompany me as long as he wasn't forced into anything.

I remember that after my life saving 'Jesus' experience, I was determined to persuade Jeff that this was the way and he needed to make a decision to follow God. I kept badgering him and badgering him. Then one day I heard the clear voice of God saying, 'Iona *stop!* Just love him and zip up the mouth.' So, I did. God draws people to himself; it wasn't for me to nag Jeff to death.

Jeff was very open, but would shut down if someone was ramming religion down his throat. So the church needed to be one that loved everyone who walked through their doors and one that was non-judgemental.

When the worship started, it was full-on clapping and hand-raising, with everything else in between. I could feel Jeff tense up initially, but after a couple of songs, he relaxed.

'Hope you come back next week guys,' it was farmer Ian standing there with two piping hot mugs of coffee for us.

I looked at Jeff.

'Yes, already looking forward to it.' Jeff took his coffee and they strolled off together discussing farming equipment. I left inspired, motivated and excited that we had found a place to worship and grow.

A week later, we were invited to another church which was literally just down the road from the farm.

I could hear our brass horse bell ringing. 'Jeff, there is someone at the door. Can you get it?'

I was in the kitchen preparing a casserole. We had just had an Aga installed and I was excited about trying out new recipes. The only issue we had with the new range was that our pets also seemed taken with it. Every mealtime, I'd have to remove three cats from the top warming plates, and I had to step around snoring dogs who had crashed out in front of the ovens. I could hear Jeff laughing and talking. An hour later, he reappeared.

'Wow. Who was that?' I asked.

'One of the local councillors, Derek. Lovely man. Had a good chat.'

'Yes, one hour. Men!'

He poured a couple of glasses of red wine and then sat down at the kitchen bench.

'He also invited us to his church.'

'Blimey, last week we couldn't find one, now it's gone up to two.'

Jeff laughed.

'It's a five-minute drive. It's a Brethren church.'

***

A year on, I was still studying. I knew now, as I had missed a few semesters because of the relocation, that it would be a five-year project, not a two-year one. I was okay with that. You can't rush learning!

Endurance had taken a back seat, partly because of my lack of enthusiasm but also due to the horrendous weather conditions. After competing in several qualifying races, I had turned my attention towards breeding and training in American Western (cowboy) riding. I was also eyeing up the possibility of competing again. We had recently purchased three quarter horses that would be ideal for my new venture. I had already been on a Western Reining course in France for ten days and loved it.

'I'm seriously considering competing in reining,' I informed Jeff.

Jeff laughed and made a funny face: 'Actually, you look like a cow girl and you act like one so, yes, sounds good!'

Reining is the Western style of dressage, but a bit more exciting, with sliding stops and spins.

'Iona will you ever stop competing?'

'It's part of my personality, so no.'

I walked towards the stables wondering, *Is this the right move? Is this what God wants me to do*? I was still doing my theology course on a part-time basis, but felt like I needed a more physical goal. I needed to pray about this.

The answer was a big fat 'No!'

35
SPINNING IN CIRCLES

I woke up and the room was spinning. I mean really spinning. I tried to sit up and I couldn't.

'Jeff, I have a problem. Everything is blurred, and the room is spinning.'

'How much did you drink last night?'

'No, this is serious. Oh no I think I'm going to be sick.' I couldn't stand, so I crawled to the bathroom. I had no idea what was happening to me. A couple of days earlier I had lost my balance walking and every now and then I would see shooting lights, but just ignored it as my imagination.

'I will ring the doctor, Iona. You stay in bed.' As he walked out towards the stairs, he turned. 'Told you it was good that we lived near the doctor's surgery.'

'Have you knocked your head recently?' asked the doctor as he pointed a light into my eyes.

'I was dancing with one of the dogs in the stable and got knocked over by accident, but that was a couple of weeks ago.'

He looked at me very strangely.

'That could be it. I think you have benign positional vertigo.'

The doctor went on to explain that this condition was triggered by the crystals in my ears having been displaced by a fall or knock. This causes a severe loss of balance and disorientation.

'It can feel like chronic sea sickness,' he explained.

He then demonstrated what they call an Epley manoeuvre, which I had to do every day, where you lie down on your back and move your head from one side to the other to try and get the crystals realigned. He also warned me that it could be something that I might have to learn to live with.

'Can you believe this! That means no reining.'

'Yes, your spinning could get a bit messy,' Jeff couldn't stop laughing. 'I'd be on the side line saying "Stop, stop," and you'd still be spinning.'

I wasn't laughing.

'Look on the bright side. You asked God for guidance and he answered *no*!'

Jeff was right. I was disappointed, but in my heart I knew that God had other plans. It was also disappointing that this had happened today. It was our wedding anniversary and we had planned a romantic dinner out. But there would be many more of those!

Jeff wandered out to help the girls hay the horses. I sat in bed just gazing out of the window that overlooked one of our horse paddocks. *Why does this keep happening to me?* I mused. From my freaky skiing accident to broken fingers, a punctured intestine to now having to live with benign positional vertigo. I had so many questions I couldn't answer. I know we live in a fallen world, but I also believe God has the last say. I do ask for guidance and I get it in a way that will stop me. God knows a simple 'no' would not be enough, so he steps in with a slightly firmer approach. Looking back, would I change any of what has happened? No!

But it just would have been nice to know what his plans were. I refocused on my natural horsemanship skills and split my time between studying, backing the young horses and working with the difficult ones on the ground. And hoped I would be able to stay away from any more hospital emergencies!

36
DIVINE INTERVENTION

Just over two years into our time in Devon we were expanding: 23 horses and two additional dogs – another Italian greyhound called Lady Bella and a 55-kilo Beauceron called Shiraz.

Animal farm!

The only frustration we had was the weather. It was continually windy, wet and cold. The summers had disappeared! Even the locals said it was bad. I used to say that the UK had only two seasons – winter and summer. Now it was just one – winter!

Jeff was now back working in Bahrain on a project, so every now and then I would escape to be with him in the sunshine, and we also managed to slot in a few hiking trips to Spain and France. But the rain in Devon was never-ending!

'Jeff, I've been thinking . . .'

He was still in Bahrain and I was out walking the four dogs in the drizzling rain.

'I hate it when you say that,' he complained.

'Ha ha! Maybe we should look at bringing Australia forward by ten years.'

'Why?'

'This weather is killing me!'

'That's a big move, Iona. Let me think about it.'

We had already decided that Australia would the best country to retire to. I knew it would be a big move, but it felt right. Not wanting to rush off in the wrong direction, I prayed for guidance. I had on so many occasions picked up on an idea that has been outside of God's plan and then hit a brick wall. Within a week, Jeff had agreed that this probably was the right time to go.

'Iona, we're right in the middle of recession, so it could take years to sell the farm, but if you start the process, we'll see what happens.'

'God will make it work, if it's meant to be.'

Silence from the other end! I know Jeff hated it when I said things like that. But God would make a way if it was right. The property was on the market for six months. In that time we had only one couple coming to look at the farm, and no sale! Things were not going to plan. I truly believed that we would have sold by this time, so much so that we had bought a farm in Australia. Thankfully, we are blessed to have the finances to do this. But what to do with Coxland farm?

'I think it's best to take it off the market, Jeff. Let's go to plan B and wait.'

Jeff was not convinced, but agreed. That same day, I was out with the dogs high up overlooking our paddocks and watching the horses grazing peacefully. I looked up at the sky and said aloud, 'God, if you want us to go to Australia, you'll need to be the estate agent. It's all up to you now.'

Within a minute, my mobile rang. It was Joanne, who lived just down the road. 'Iona, we have some friends over. Can we come and visit the horses sometime today?'

'Yes, I'm here. This afternoon is good for me.'

It was good to see Joanne and meet her friends, plus all their kids. We did a complete tour of the farm and the children were ecstatic as they could pat and stroke the horses. Nearing the end of their visit, to my absolute amazement, the couple asked if the farm was for sale.

I nearly fell over backwards. I tried not to be over enthusiastic about their interest and managed to stay super cool.

A day later, they had put in an offer for the farm. I was stunned and so was Jeff. But it wasn't what we had hoped for.

'Iona, we cannot accept that price. We do need to break even.'

Jeff was right. We didn't need to make a profit, but we did need to cover all the renovation costs.

'They may come back with a higher offer?' I felt optimistic. Then, from out of the blue, I got a phone call from the couple who had seen the farm six months earlier. They had heard someone was trying to buy the property and wanted to outbid them. What? They offered the asking price, and the deal was done, sold. Jeff and I sat looking at each other.

'Can you believe that just happened?' Jeff was astounded.

'No, I'm still in shock,' I agreed. 'But I did ask God to intervene, and he did.'

Jeff nodded, 'I think he did!'

Two weeks ago, we had taken the property of the market. Today we had sold it without an estate agent!

'Iona, you need to start planning. This is a mega-move and we need to make some serious decisions,' said Jeff. We sat and talked for hours about the logistics of the move and which of the animals we would take with us.

I stood looking out of our bedroom window. This was all amazing, but also heart wrenching. We had decided to take only four of the twenty-three horses. The three we had bred and Charlie the palomino. The cost of transporting even one horse was crazy, so we had no choice. Our retired racehorses were sent to Thierry and Silvia in France, so they could live out their days in sunshine, the older horses were euthanized and the others were gifted to friends. This was tough!

Another sad event was saying a final goodbye to Obelix. He had been diagnosed with cancer a couple of months earlier and was beginning to suffer.

We were excited about our new beginning, but it came with a price. Saying farewell. We were leaving a community we loved. We were leaving a house we had put our heart and soul into restoring. But this still felt right.

A new start awaited.

37
MONK IMPRESSIONS

It was a smooth transition. Two forty-foot containers, two cats, three dogs and four horses from one side of the world to the other, and not one hiccup.

Australia was a totally different lifestyle – for me anyway. Jeff just slotted back in to living down under. As we'd also bought the adjacent farm to our first purchase, we now had two properties side by side and were living in the new one whilst it was being renovated. It was a busy time managing 270 acres and settling in all the animals, but we loved the challenge.

We were standing at the top of the ridge overlooking our two properties. The dogs were running around chasing each other and just being really goofy. They were happy. *This is absolutely stunning*, I thought.

Our farms were located near a small village called Chillingham, in northern New South Wales. The farms were situated in a caldera, a large, bowl-shaped volcanic depression, surrounded by mountain ranges and sub-tropical rain forest. With the renowned Gold Coast only forty minutes away, we had the best of countryside and beaches. Plus, we had Jeff's mum Judy and stepfather Neil living on our first farm. What more could you ask for!

'Iona, Jeff said you would take me to church on Sunday?' Judy informed me.

'Did he really, that's nice of him,' I sighed. 'I'll think about it!'

I knew Judy wanted to go to the Anglican church in Murwillumbah, but I was wanting a to go to a more informal charismatic one. However, I knew I really had no choice in the matter.

As Judy and I strolled into the church the following Sunday, I quickly realized the service was halfway through. I grabbed Judy's arm and swung around to make a quick exit.

'No, stay. You're not going anywhere!'

We were ambushed by two elderly ladies, who proceeded to tell us that two services had combined so the start time had changed. I looked around at the aged congregation. I must have been the youngest by years. And more years! But this was good for Judy. My convent memories came flooding back as I sat there on the rock-hard pew. It was what I would call bordering on high church: rituals and traditions. I had a gut feeling that God was telling me that this is where he wanted me to be. *No, this is not for me. Great for Judy, but no way for me. Not even up for debate. Sorry!* I told God.

The more time I spent in prayer, reading scripture and just sitting in God's presence, the better I became at discerning his voice. But sometimes it wasn't what I wanted to hear. After the service, we were invited to join everyone for coffee and biscuits.

'Hi, I hear you used to live in Dubai?'

I turned to see a smiling lady, who introduced herself as Kate.

'Yes, we did, then France, then the UK, and now here.'

'I have a very dear friend who works over in Dubai, his name is Paul Trelor and he works with horses.'

I looked at her thinking, *no way that's bizarre!*

'He's one of our closest friends.'

We had many friends in Dubai, but Paul was one of our closest. This was wacky. Was this confirmation? Maybe, but one that I didn't agree with. We chatted for an hour until Judy started tugging at my arm. Time for home.

I came back from church thinking maybe it was worth another try, plus it would be good to see Kate again. The following Sunday I dragged Jeff along. And like me the previous week, he stood rigid, while doing a stunned mullet impression. I could see he wasn't convinced. But over the weeks, he warmed to the people, as did I. We also befriended the vicar, Bruce. It wasn't long before Jeff and he were the best of friends. Things moved fairly rapidly from there.

It was another sunny Sunday. Even though the high street was quiet, the cafés were heaving in Murwillumbah. Revd Bruce and Jeff were cracking silly jokes while I just chilled. I was loving this climate.

'Iona, Jeff tells me you have just finished a course in biblical studies?'

'Yep, it was a two-year course that took me five.'

I could tell Bruce was looking a bit more serious.

'Have you ever thought about becoming a licensed lay minister?'

I nearly choked on my biscuit.

'The simple answer to that is no!' I was laughing inside. *He's definitely barking up the wrong tree here!*

'We could really do with someone like you to help us.'

Not wanting to be rude, I said I would think about it. I could not imagine myself in a white robe in an Anglican church following all the rules, no way! But as the weeks went on, Bruce kept asking. In the end, I agreed to start the process, believing that my qualifications would not be acceptable, and that God would close the doors. Months went by, and still no response from the powers that be. Bruce was getting very upset, but I was at peace knowing that if it wasn't to be, God had another route in mind.

Then one morning the phone rang. 'Hello Bruce, what can I do for you?'

'Great news, the bishop has agreed,' he informed me.

That was a bolt from the blue. I really believed that this had all gone away, but no. Now I was embarking on a training programme on the ins and outs of becoming a lay minister. I knew I was going to have problems conforming, so I just took it day by day and step by step.

'Iona what have you done to your robe?' asked Madeline, one of the other lay ministers. I'd gone off to a tailor to have a white robe made but had added a few things.

'Well we have splits either side for ventilation, a kangaroo pouch for my tissues and lip salve and a hood. I like hoodies.'

'But you look more like a monk!' Madeline was laughing.

'Jeff says I look like a cross between a garden gnome and an angel.'

We laughed.

I did struggle with all the dos and the do nots, with what was the right way and what was the wrong way. It was character building, I suppose. And I wasn't the only one who was conforming. Since our arrival, Bruce had questioned Jeff about his faith and what he believed. Jeff, in return, would normally crack a joke. That's his way of changing the subject. But then one day it all changed. I was sitting with Judy and Neil out on their veranda watching the parakeets and cockatoos playing in the water feeder. Jeff was on the phone.

'Who were you speaking to?' I asked him when he had finished.

'Only Bruce.'

Jeff went inside to prepare the customary gin and tonics for Judy and me, while Neil had his beer and Jeff returned to make his rum and coke. We all sat in silence watching the wildlife. We had planted an orchard directly in front of their house: apples, oranges, avocados and more. The birds were flitting from the water feeder to the orchard.

'I've decided to get confirmed,' Jeff suddenly announced.

We all turned, stunned to look at Jeff. Bruce had been persistent in trying to persuade Jeff to make a commitment.

'Bruce said that the bishop is coming in a couple of weeks, so I have decided it's time. Time to commit.'

'Wow, Jeff, that's great news.' I went up and gave him a big hug. Judy had tears in her eyes. Neil wasn't even sure what confirmation was and carried on drinking his beer. I thought to myself, *We have travelled all the way across the world and now Jeff is taking a step that will change his life dramatically.* Even with this decision, I was still concerned that a traditional church would not be the right place for us to grow. But we had to trust God.

***

I was standing in the sanctuary looking out across the pews at all the smiling faces. This was my first Sunday service as a lay minister at All Saints Church. I assisted Bruce in reading from the service sheet and administering the wine at communion. As a lay minister, I was able to carry out all priestly duties except take weddings and bless the sacraments. My friends in the convent school would be rolling around hysterically if they could see me now. *I'm not sure if I'm ever going to be comfortable with this,* I thought. *It's too formal.* Thankfully, there was soon to be an opportunity to move to a more informal gathering.

Jeff and I walked into St John's Church. It was the last church standing in Tyalgum; all the others had closed.

'What a beautiful little church,' said Jeff. 'You can feel the presence of God in here.'

'Wow, yes, you're right,' I agreed. 'How special.'

It was bursting with character but was a little worn around the edges. The wooden-clad church was pale cream, green and red, with old wooden pews, arched doorways, a cosy sanctuary and a bell tower. It could probably seat a hundred at a push. This was one of three Anglican churches that Bruce looked after. He didn't seem very interested in it, so Jeff and I offered to step in and help. It was also only a ten-minute drive from the farm. This was our first Sunday attending the service. We sat at the front and waited for the rest of the congregation to arrive. We waited . . . and waited . . .

In total, we were five, three of whom were over 80 years old. Even though the numbers were few, it didn't matter, I knew this was where Jeff and I should be. It was going to be a challenge, but we were ready.

The quirky rural village of Tyalgum with a population of around 500 had an olde worlde feel about it. The small, picturesque high street oozed personality, with its boutique country art and craft shops, with the centrepiece being the Flutterbies Cottage Café. This versatile café offered homemade delicacies, hosted pizza evenings, live music, dancing and Shakespearian theatrical entertainment. This thriving village was also host to several iconic music and literary festivals during the year. So, while the village was booming, St John's Church stood alone, lacking tender loving care. *This was going to be an interesting mission!*

'Iona, I am more than happy for you to take the church services, but would you also like to be the churchwarden at Tyalgum?' asked Bruce.

I didn't even stop to think: 'Why yes, if that helps St John's.'

An hour later, I rang Kate to ask, 'What does a church warden do?'

'Why?'

'I just said yes to being one and have no idea what that means.' We laughed.

'A churchwarden looks after the building and its grounds and also oversees everything to do with the church. Plus, you'll be on the Parish Council.'

Kate had also agreed to come and support us at the one service a month we had at Tyalgum. I was now on a mission. Committees are not my forte, but I felt more relaxed when Jeff took on the role of rector's warden, which meant he'd also be on the council. Good to have a partner in crime. I can see why people laugh and joke about church committees because the Christian spirit goes out of the window and politics takes over. At our first council meeting, I was blown away with the antics and underhand comments. Jeff and I did try throwing in a few jokes to lighten the proceedings but I think we made it worse.

Our monthly service at Tyalgum was like a breath of fresh air. I was given free rein to mix traditional and charismatic together, which gave it a more laid back and relaxed ambiance. Three months into taking over at St John's, we were up to twenty people in the congregation, from a range of denominations. It was a community – one that was growing.

We sat around the table looking at each other. Another jolly, fun evening at the Parish Council meeting. They were painful. I had just put forward a proposal for a second service at Tyalgum. Once a month was not enough, especially as we were expanding. Normally we'd vote, but unfortunately it never got that far. Bruce totally stunned me when he stated, 'No, it's not going to happen!' No discussion.

I walked away that night seething and angry. I had worked hard to get St John's back on track. There didn't seem to be any logic behind Bruce's decision. I was tired and felt a bit like an octopus being pulled in all directions. I was running around doing my lay minister's roles, churchwarden's duties, looking after all the public relations and helping with computer presentations. The decision not to expand St John's with a second service floored me. I just couldn't understand it.

The next morning, I decided to stop saying 'yes' to everything and take a few steps backwards. In my heart, I felt God say 'back away' and so I did. I resigned as churchwarden and public relations manager that day. Bruce was devastated. I chose to ignore his emails and calls, as I was still angry and I may have said something I'd regret later. I didn't want to jeopardize our friendship because of my temper. It was best to stay away. When I was finally ready to see Bruce, he was more than apologetic, and his humility was heartfelt.

'I am sorry Bruce, but I took on too much. I am happy to be a lay minister but that's it. I need some balance in my life,' I explained.

'Sure, I understand, and we'll talk soon about a second service.'

We hugged and made up.

Taking a step back proved to be a good move for me. I had been so wrapped up in doing stuff for the church, it had affected my time with God in the morning and also the training of the horses. Now I could balance it all out.

But then a spanner was thrown into the works, completely out of the blue!

38
ON STEROIDS

It was coming up to Christmas 2013 and I was having a spring-cleaning session in my office, which is a rare event, but I had books and paperwork everywhere. I do get stressed when the house or my office looks untidy, so this was a wise move. But I was distracted, as I could see Jeff was on the phone, pacing up and down on the veranda. It looked intense. I wondered who he was talking to.

'You look happy,' I said to Jeff as he strolled into the office followed by all three dogs.

'Yes. You won't believe this, but I've just been offered a consultancy job.' I could see the spark of excitement in Jeff's eyes. His work was his passion and I knew he was struggling with retirement.

'Wow, that's great news!'

'The only problem is that it's based in Dubai.'

I froze.

'You're kidding me?'

'Nope. It looks like I will be away two weeks of every month. What do you think?'

We spent the evening talking it over. It was hard to take in, as we'd only been in Australia for four months. I knew in my heart that this was what Jeff wanted, but was this part of God's plan?

Maybe this was divine intervention, I thought. Jeff is not a farmer. Every time he went out on the tractor, I worried for his safety and that of anyone he met on his travels. In France he was not allowed to drive the tractor and in Devon he spent most of his time in the ditch or stuck in mud or taking out one of the horse fences. Plus, I remember the time he came down the lane with our massive cherry picker and forgot to lower the fork and almost took out the electricity and telephone cables.

In a situation like this, all you can do is ask for divine guidance. We both felt at peace that this was a good opportunity for Jeff, even though I wasn't convinced he'd be returning every month. But as I had two helpers on the farm, it also meant that I could travel to Dubai if Jeff wasn't able to return. Did I want to do this? No. When I left Dubai in 2006, I swore that I would never return. The desert was being eaten up by skyscrapers and the roads were a nightmare. Every day it was becoming more like an adult Disneyland. A week into our decision, I was asking God why this was happening and how this was going to help Jeff's faith. Then I remembered.

'Jeff, last year just before we left Devon, Pauline and Michael gave me the telephone number of Michael's goddaughter who is married to a minister in Dubai,' I reminded him.

'Yes, I remember. She said we should make contact.'

'I have an email with all their details, so I'll dig it out.'

Pauline and Michael were missionaries and had become very close friends. At the time, I thought it a bit weird when she sent me an email with Pete and Liz's Dubai contact details, especially as we had left Dubai seven years earlier and were now relocating to Australia.

'I think it's a very charismatic church Jeff, but there's no harm trying it out,' I said.

In my heart, I had a feeling this would be good for Jeff.

'Jeff you promise me you'll go?'

No answer.

'No church, no Dubai!'

We laughed.

A couple of months later, Jeff was in Dubai overseeing the development of the Palazzi Versace Hotel. He was loving his work, but what about church?

It was another glorious day and I was out riding with Beatrice who worked for us. I was on Zara, a pure-bred Arabian that Jeff had bought me from the people we'd bought the second farm from, and Beatrice was riding Ibn, Jeff's new chestnut Arab that he had been given as a gift. We were now up to seven horses, with these two new additions and an old mare that had been left behind on the property. We were trotting up along the ridge, heading towards our forest, which was a maze of good riding tracks. I heard my phone go beep. I knew it was a message from Jeff. That morning he had gone along to Gateway Church in Dubai, so this was feedback time. I slowed up, pulled my phone out and read the message.

'It's like Crediton Congregational Church but on steroids!' he reported.

I started laughing, but wasn't sure if this was a good sign or not. Later that evening we skyped each other.

'It's fairly full-on with dancing, clapping and singing, plus it's not a one-hour service but two hours.'

'Sounds amazing. Did you meet Pete and Liz?'

'Yes, everybody is very friendly. They must have more than eighty different nationalities at the church. You'll see for yourself when you come over next month.'

Jeff's promise of returning to Australia on a monthly basis never materialized, which was no surprise. So I was the one who travelling backwards and forwards. Jeff had rented a small two-bedroom apartment overlooking the centre of Dubai, and the world's tallest building, the Burj Khalifa. It was awesome, except for travelling in the apartment lifts. I am slightly claustrophobic, so 54 floors in a lift is a long way. Thankfully, the lifts were fast, so I never had time to worry. My first visit back to Dubai felt weird, but I opted to forget the old Dubai and treat this as a new city. My focus now was on Gateway Church and meeting up with Jeff's new friends.

There must have been more than four hundred people in the Holiday Inn's ballroom. The atmosphere was electric. This was my first worship service. Yes, it was very 'happy clappy' but there was a strong sense of God's presence. For the two hours, I felt like I had been transported to heaven and back. I was overwhelmed emotionally. This was all very new to me, I'd never really experienced church like this.

I was disappointed to find out out that the church did not use women in leadership roles or to preach. I asked Pete, the minister, about it and he explained that this was the theology of Regions Beyond, the group of churches of which Gateway was a part.

Despite my disappointment, I felt God say that this was the right church for now. I still found it rather strange, because when I was in Australia, I'd had a full-on schedule of preaching, leading worship and hosting Bible studies, yet now in Dubai I wouldn't be able to do most of these things. But it gave me time to worship and focus on my relationship with God without taking on extra responsibility, so perhaps God was using this time to slow me down.

I now became the one to bounce back and forth between Australia and Dubai for two months at a time. It was great for the air miles but hard to establish any kind of routine.

Even though Jeff's visits to Australia were rare, he never missed a family get-together. One such event was my father's eightieth birthday party. It had become a family tradition that every five years we would get together on his birthday. It had started on his seventieth, when the whole family descended on us in France, and then his seventy-fifth was in Devon. Again, it seemed that wherever Jeff and I were was where he wanted his party. Not that we are socialites, but we can host a good shindig. On this occasion, all the stops were pulled out. Daddy and Kathleen had a month with us, as they had flown in from their home in the US. They were happy to chill out in our small guest cottage, which allowed them to escape from the banter and noise of his daughters and sons-in-law.

One of the funniest memories is of Kathleen arriving at the main house on the first morning looking a bit stressed.

'I am sorry Iona, your dad has set fire to the kettle.'

'How on earth did he do that?' I said.

She held out a charred kettle.

'He didn't realize it was an electric kettle and he put it on the gas to heat up!'

Jeff and I couldn't stop laughing.

'As he's the birthday boy, we'll forgive him,' said Jeff. 'At least the cottage is still standing.'

It was a wonderful family time, but we were all very aware that my father's health had deteriorated considerably. He had started to drift off to bed just after 7 p.m., which was not like him. I think we all guessed that something was amiss.

39
RENEWED

I stood looking at the inflatable swimming pool. We were in Geetha and Jacob's back garden with Jeff and several others who were to be baptised. I had previously had the romantic notion that this would be happening at the Jordan River in Israel. But no, here we were in sunny Dubai in a back garden. Jacob, one of the church elders, and Fusi, one of the other ministers, were carrying out the baptisms.

Jeff and I had been baptised as infants, but felt strongly that it's a decision people should consciously make themselves. Many evangelical churches bless babies, and they baptise by full immersion only when the person is old enough to declare their own decision to follow Christ. After our two-weekend introduction course as new members of Gateway Church, we were given the option. It felt right, and I knew this would be a life-changing moment. We were ready to dedicate our lives to Christ.

Jeff was baptised first and then he was asked by Fusi if he wanted to help him baptise me. They stood either side of me and Fusi asked, 'Iona do you want to receive Jesus as your Lord and Saviour?'

'Yes, I do,' I replied.

'Do you believe that Jesus came, suffered death and rose again for your sins?'

'Yes, I do.'

'Then I baptise you in the name of the Father, the Son and the Holy Spirit.'

Next minute I was under water, held for a moment and then lifted back up. Later I found out that while I was under the water Jeff had suggested to Fusi that maybe they could leave me under! Australian sense of humour.

I stood with my eyes closed while one of the elders prayed over me and spoke: 'Iona, now be bold and courageous and speak. Speak of what God has done in your life.' It felt like Jesus was speaking directly to me.

Considering the dramatic way God had been working in my life, I was expecting some great surge of spirit-filled emotion that would leave me all warm and fuzzy after the baptism. The words spoke to me, but I had been expecting more. After a quick change of clothes, some refreshments and some friendly banter, we went back to our apartment.

'How do you feel?' I asked Jeff.

'No different. And you?'

'No, the same – no different.'

We couldn't help but see the funny side of this and burst out laughing. We stepped into the apartment and I suddenly had this overwhelming sense of peace, plus I suddenly felt really tired. It felt like I had just run a marathon. Not in a bad sense, it was a good tired, and it wasn't only me.

'I think I need to lie down,' Jeff said as he headed towards the stairs.

'I'll join you.'

Five hours later, I woke up. Jeff was still sleeping. It was a seriously deep sleep. I vaguely remember at one point waking up to see my right arm reaching up to the ceiling. It all seemed very bizarre – or was it a dream? It didn't feel like a dream. That weekend we did nothing. Actually, we were both totally exhausted; our bodies were heavy and tired but we both had a real sense of peace.

Our apartment was in the middle of Dubai's financial district, which gave us unlimited choices in cafés and restaurants. I was sitting in Café Nero, mulling over the weekend. For the last year, I had enjoyed the preaching and I loved the speaking opportunities, so the words spoken at my baptism resonated deeply with me. I knew it was time to talk about my life, and how, through God's grace and patience, he had never once abandoned me. I silently prayed while drinking my coffee, 'Father, I know those words have come from you, but how, when and where do I speak?'

My mobile beeped. I read the message and nearly fell off my chair. It was Chad, an Anglican deacon from the Gold Coast, Australia asking if I was available to speak and give my testimony at one of the largest Anglican schools in Queensland. I was absolutely knocked sideways; I could not believe what had just happened.

But it wasn't all plain sailing.

40
WARFARE

Back in Australia, I stood on stage looking out at more than sixty students. This was to be the first of two classes I would talk to that day. Chad introduced me, and I began my forty-minute talk on my life as a professional skier and horse rider, and how God had stepped in to show me a better way of living. After each talk, we had a question and answer session. By the end of the morning I was exhausted, but happy. I enjoyed sharing my experiences and felt God had planted some seeds. Now is was time to go home and rest.

I was on a high as I drove through the gates of the farm. The dogs came bounding out to greet me. But where was Be Bop? I went into the house but there was no sign of him there. Then I went out the back to my office.

'There you are!'

He was curled up on the couch but not moving. I immediately knew something was wrong. He had been diagnosed with a tumour two years earlier, but we had managed with surgery and medication to keep him in good health. I rolled him over and saw a massive swelling where the tumour had originally been.

I leapt back into the car with Be Bop in my arms. He was barely moving. I called through to the vets who were a thirty-minute drive away. As I walked into the surgery, they quickly took him, and I went to sit down in a private waiting room. I was distraught and bewildered. I'd had such a good morning. Having the opportunity to tell my story had left me feeling energized and elated. And now this! Jeff and I are probably overly passionate about our pets, but they are our family and we love each of them dearly. Helen the veterinary nurse came in carrying little Be Bop.

'Iona, we are sorry but the cancer has spread throughout his whole body.'

'But I don't understand, yesterday he was in perfect health?'

'Yes, it's strange that there were no warning signs.'

We agreed that it was best to put him down. I would have one last night with him and then I would bring him back in the morning. I drove home in shock. *God, why? How could you let this happen?*

It was a sad week. I felt like a small part of me had left. Be Bop was such a special little fellow. This was heart wrenching. The following week I was back at the Lindisfarne Anglican School for a morning session with two other classes. As I drove home, it felt as if the dark cloud hovering over me was lifting. I was still feeling slightly gloomy, but the morning with the students bought a glow to my heart and a feeling of peace.

As I was driving up the farm driveway, I could see Beatrice waving her arms frantically, directing me towards the stables instead of the house.

'What's wrong?' I called.

Beatrice was on the washstand with our 3-year-old mare Kismet.

'She can't walk. Her front leg is badly swollen,' Beatrice informed me.

I took one look and realized we needed to call Greg, our horse vet.

I walked back towards the house to let the dogs out. I felt under attack. I could not believe this had happened on the same day as my talks – again. Was I missing something? Greg arrived within the hour, and Kismet was diagnosed with a severe abscess in her foot and the infection had travelled up her leg. He was surprised we hadn't spotted it earlier. Beatrice was adamant, as was I, that Kismet had shown no signs of an infection. Kismet was moved to a smaller paddock, so she could start a three-week course of medication to help reduce the inflammation.

My third and final visit to Lindisfarne was amazing. We had a real breakthrough with the older children. I was going to miss my weekly visits but was excited to see what other speaking opportunities would come from this. But my joy turned into absolute horror, when I returned home.

Shiraz, our Beauceron, and Samson, our new Rottweiler puppy, came bounding up to greet me, but no Lady Bella. I chose not to think about the last two weeks and went searching. I found her under my office table foaming at the mouth and having seizures.

'This cannot be happening! No way is this happening! What on earth is going on?' I screamed.

'Beatrice, call the vets please and tell them I have another emergency. I'll be there in less than twenty minutes. Thanks.'

I picked Bella up, jumped back into the car and drove like a maniac. She was on the passenger seat. I had one hand on the wheel and the other one on her while she was fitting and foaming. Every now and then she would just go rigid. I was crying and screaming. Now I was angry, really angry with God. If he was in control of everything, then he must have allowed this to happen.

'Why God? Why?' I screamed. 'This is the third week in a row. You've got to be kidding me! I stand on stage and tell those children about the love you have for them, and then this. What's going on?'

I could feel my heart being ripped open, and at that moment I saw God as the one who had caused this. The vets were waiting for me as I screeched to a halt outside the clinic. They were also slightly taken aback that in ten days I had lost Be Bop and it looked like the same was going to happen to Bella. They rushed her into the emergency room and sat me in a quiet room.

I sat shaking. I looked back over the last couple of weeks. I couldn't understand what was happening. Had I done something wrong? Was it me? I was hoping I would wake up; this must be a bad dream.

After about ten minutes, Helen came in shaking her head. 'We have no idea what's happened to her. Her vital signs are very weak and she's fading. It's not looking good. The only option is to transport her to the specialist vets on the Gold Coast.'

'Okay let do that,' I begged.

'Iona, she is gravely ill. She may not survive the trip.'

I wasn't, at this stage, prepared to lose another pet and I believed in my heart that God could turn this situation around. Bella left in the pet ambulance, and I drove home. The emergency unit would contact me when she arrived.

The phone calls bounced backwards and forwards between the vets and our house, but even after hours of trying to stabilize her, she appeared to be losing the battle. At midnight I got the call I was dreading, saying that she didn't have long but that there was one option that might give her a chance, and that was to put her on a ventilator. This would allow her to fight what was happening inside her while the ventilator did the breathing. But it came with a price tag! I quickly called Jeff and we made the decision to proceed. Even with this possibility of keeping her alive, we all knew there was still only a slim chance that she would survive. Now it was a waiting game.

The next day the vet called: 'She's fighting really hard to live. We're going to keep her on the ventilator for another couple of hours. I cannot promise anything.'

By mid-morning, I was emotionally exhausted. I could not focus on anything; I just sat and waited. I asked God continually why this was happening. I knew that we lived in a broken world, and that even though we are under God's sovereignty, evil spirits are also very real. I prayed for wisdom and begged him to save Bella.

Finally, that afternoon there was a breakthrough. The vet called in a state of absolute elation saying, 'It's a miracle!' Bella was off the machine, breathing and sitting up.

After a week of Bella being in intensive care, I arrived at the Gold Coast hospital to be reunited with her. As they brought her out into reception, she ran towards me and leapt into my arms. The waiting area was full, so I was determined not to be an emotional wreck. But I was. I didn't really have to feel embarrassed, though, as everyone else also seemed to be crying.

During those three weeks, I learnt a great deal. Afterwards, my dear friend Kate came and sat with me for hours and hours, teaching me about the very real world of spiritual warfare. If she had spoken to me about it before all this happened, I would have dismissed her words as fantasy. But having both physically and emotionally come face to face with evil, I listened. I came to realize that the devil will try anything to stop people hearing the truth. He tried to stop me sharing my story by targeting something that meant a great deal to me – my pets.

After my three weeks of turmoil, I began to look at life from a totally different perspective. I now understood that there are invisible forces all around us trying to thwart what we do for God. Being aware of this, was I still up for the challenge?

41
RAMBO ARRIVES

My next public speaking engagement was in Sydney, where I was the guest speaker at a lady's conference.

'Are you sure you want to do this, Iona. Remember what happened last time?' Jeff was being half-serious and half-funny, I think!

'Yes, but now I know what I'm up against. I have to pray for protection.' I put my arms around him and gave him a gentle hug. 'Are you worried something's going to happen to you?'

'Yes, it has crossed my mind. He's targeted the dogs and the horses. It's either me or the cat next.'

We laughed.

The Sydney conference was a great success and we had no incidents except that I partially lost my voice. But on stage with a microphone I managed fine. As soon as I arrived back at the farm, my voice was back to normal. It was almost funny.

Back on the farm, all had returned to normal except Lady Bella, who seemed at a real loss. She and Be Bop had been inseparable. I needed to find her a new friend.

'I have searched the whole of Australia and not one Italian Greyhound,' I complained.

Jeff was playing solitaire on his iPad. No answer.

'I spoke to the animal rescue people and they suggested a whippet,' I continued.

Still no feedback. So, I took that as confirmation to proceed. I scrolled through the internet until I found the perfect whippet. I contacted the breeder who had a six-month-old for sale. He was called Rambo and was supposedly trained and very quiet. I did think at the time that Rambo was a strange name for the personality she was describing.

Rambo was flying in from Melbourne. So, Jeff and I drove to the Gold Coast Airport to collect him. We followed the security guard around the back to the cargo area.

'Here's Rambo,' the guard pointed to a large container.

'That's not a whippet. He's more like a full-size Greyhound,' groaned Jeff.

I peered into the travel cage.

'Wow he *is* very big!'

But what could we do? Nothing! We renamed him Bruce, which totally suited his personality. I have never in my life come across a dog that was so destructive; he ate everything. His trick was he would chew the last thing you touched as you left the room, which could be the TV remote control, a pencil, a hairbrush, even a table. He wasn't fussy. His other two tricks were jumping out of the dog run and, when walking, if we let him off the lead he would take off at a full gallop and go for about a kilometre. Sometimes we didn't see him again for an hour or more. The lesson here is don't buy a dog on the internet. So, I started praying for guidance. And my prayer was soon answered. My sister Alison, an avid dog lover, came to stay and fell in love with Bruce.

'He is so handsome. I do love his personality,' said Alison as we were out walking the four dogs across the hay field. Today Bruce had decided not to do a runner. He was on his best behaviour.

'If you ever want to rehome him, please let me know. He'd fit in really well with our gang.'

Not wanting to appear overly eager to get rid of him, I waited twelve hours before accepting her offer. Don't get me wrong, I love dogs, but I believe it's important to match owners with their dogs. Years on, Bruce is happy in his forever home. Well Bruce is, not sure about Alison. We were now back to three dogs. It was sad to see him go, but at least Bruce had stayed within the family.

Shortly after his departure, we had a call with some bad news. Dad had called to say that he had been diagnosed with colon cancer and that he was expected to have three years or less to live. We had all realized that he was unwell, but we weren't expecting this. I was in deep thought as we soared over the city of Brisbane heading back to Dubai. My father's sickness had left our whole family in shock. Life seemed so fragile!

I sat in our ultra-modern open-plan apartment overlooking the Sheikh's palaces, the Zabeel Racing Stables and the tallest building in the world, watching as the sun popped its head up over the distant dunes. It was another stunning sunrise. Here my thoughts went back to my dad's illness. Time just seemed to tick by. I had nothing to do except think. It was like the world had stopped! I couldn't remember the last time I'd had no work commitments or projects or goals to complete. I'd retired from horseracing, I had no church duties to perform in Dubai, and I'd completed my theology course.

What I did have was time: time to talk with God and be in his presence. The days were full of peace, stillness and tranquillity. In the evenings, Jeff and I sat on the balcony having dinner and watching the sparkling lights of Dubai below.

'Iona, what are you going to do or should I say, what would you like to do?'

That was the big question.

'To be honest, I have no idea. I'm praying about that, but nothing yet.'

Jeff smiled and said, 'You need to pray harder.' He laughed.

I knew in my heart that the time would come when God would open a door. I just needed to be patient and wait. But after several weeks, I was beginning to get itchy feet. One morning, in desperation I got on my knees and cried out, 'Whatever it takes Lord, whatever it takes. I will do whatever you want.'

Nothing!

But I knew he was listening.

42
WHATEVER IT TAKES

A month later, I had just arrived back into Dubai after a short break in Australia. Jeff had arranged for me to meet Raza Jafar, one of his philanthropist friends, for lunch. He had a project that he thought I might be interested in taking on.

'We are looking for someone to co-ordinate a new global anti-slavery initiative which I'm working on with the Church of England and the Vatican,' explained Raza. 'Jeff was telling me about your public relations and marketing background and your work with the church. Thought you might be interested.'

We spent the next couple of hours discussing Raza's plans and what he hoped to achieve. I can't say I was jumping up and down with excitement. After 15 hours on a plane, then being bombarded with information, I felt rather dazed by it all. I made no commitment. I didn't have any enthusiasm for it and I wasn't sure this was the path that God had planned for me. So, I prayed that doors would be closed if it wasn't the right way and for the doors to be opened if this was his will. Well, the doors kept opening, and the meetings kept happening. So I went with the flow. Going back into the corporate world was not what I'd had in mind when I prayed, 'Whatever it takes, Lord. I will do whatever it takes!'

But it was where God wanted me – in Dubai working on this new initiative. My first task was to co-ordinate a high-profile event with twenty prominent entrepreneurs and philanthropists at Lambeth Palace in London to kick-start the initiative. My heart was sold on the project when I listened to Archbishop of Canterbury Justin Welby talk about the importance of having a servant heart. He also stressed that if any of us were in it for ourselves, then the project would fail. Lord Bishop Alastair, who was leading the Church of England on this project, also stressed the importance of humility as an attribute to help push this cause forward. In addition, the Vatican's Bishop Sanchez's talk on how the Beatitudes should be prominent in this initiative and this all enabled me to see God's face in the campaign.

As the months went by, my role got busier and busier as the newly named Global Sustainability Network grew in members and staged events. But as it got more hectic, so did my stress levels. I had many anxious days, where I felt my brain was going to implode with the amount of stuff I had to do. It had been a long while since I had been in this type of environment. Trying to keep the Church of England, the Vatican and Raza happy wasn't easy.

It was 8 a.m. and Jeff had just left for work. I stood hanging over the balcony railings looking down at the apartment swimming pool. I felt miserable. I wasn't sure I could do another day with GSN. No, I wasn't contemplating jumping, I was just depressed. The weather was also gloomy, heavy clouds hung over the city – a rare sight for Dubai. I looked up and cried, 'God I'm really struggling. I'm not made for a role like this.'

Suddenly a ray of sunlight light popped up around a cloud and shone down directly onto my face. I felt a warmth and his presence. I felt God say, 'I am with you. I know what you're going through, and I understand.' I needed this reassurance. God knew what I was feeling, and he had it all in hand. That same week, at church I felt God speak directly to me when the pastor quoted Colossians 4:17 (NIV), 'See to it that you complete the ministry you have received in the Lord.' That was telling me!

For the next fourteen months, I lived and breathed the Global Sustainability Network, which was slowly becoming a solid organization that was making a massive difference in the world. We established regular forums at Lambeth Palace in London, the Vatican in Rome, Dubai, and the United Nations in New York, bringing together global entrepreneurs, philanthropists and change-makers who were passionate about eradicating modern-day slavery, organ trafficking and child prostitution. The list of GSN members was starting to read like a who's who in *Forbes* magazine but, leaving status aside, each one came to unite and work in partnership, offering their skills and expertise.

I was becoming increasingly aggravated and frustrated, as there was a great deal of talk and not enough action. Plus, I was struggling with all the egos – including my own. But we now had a solid management team in place and after a definite 'It's okay to go' from God, I resigned from my post. I was burnt-out and exhausted. It was time to move on. But I still stayed on as a member of GSN.

Another factor in my decision to leave GSN was that I had also been accepted onto an online degree course in theology with Ridley College in Melbourne. I knew it would have been impossible to co-ordinate GSN and study full time.

It was also at this time that we decided to move out of the apartment in Dubai and back to Desert Palms Polo and Country Club, where we used to have the horses. It gave us more space and we needed to spread out a little as the apartment was beginning to feel very claustrophobic.

***

Space was the one thing I didn't have to worry about in Australia. I walked into my office. The dogs were sunning themselves by the large sliding glass doors. I had just finished working Shalom and Tango in the arena. Now it was time to study. I looked around the room. It looked like a student's den and an art studio rolled into one – easels, paints, boxes and books. I had taken up painting again using airbrushing techniques, so I could transform large canvases into abstract biblical artworks. I was sitting there at my desk just taking in the glorious surroundings of our farm when my mobile rang 'Oh Happy Day'. And yes, today was another one of those days.

'Iona, Bishop Sarah would like to meet you regarding your application to start training for ordination. Can you give her a ring? She is expecting a call this afternoon,' explained Revd Bruce.

'Yes, will do. Wow that was a quick response!'

'You're fortunate, she just happened to be passing through.'

It had felt like a natural progression to go from a lay minister to getting ordained as a priest, which was another reason for embarking on the degree course. But before the official procedure started, I had to be interviewed by the bishop to get her to approve me as a suitable candidate.

'I think I'll come with you,' suggested Jeff. 'I've always wanted to meet a lady bishop.'

'You'll have to behave. No funny comments,' I warned.

Bishop Sarah had made history several months earlier, when she was chosen to be the first female bishop in Australia. I was also intrigued to meet her too. If you want good coffee and French homemade cakes, the Blue Frog in Murwillumbah, run by friends André and Gilles, was the place to be. And here the three of us sat; it was relaxed and casual. Bishop Sarah was kind, humble, articulate and funny. After the friendly introductions, we sat down, and Bishop Sarah said, 'The first thing I want to know Iona is, are you after my job?'

I laughed.

Jeff answered for me, 'Probably!'

'No, that's one thing you won't have to worry about,' I assured her.

It was a very informal interview, so much so that I walked away feeling like I'd made a friend. Now I just needed to wait for Bishop Sarah's approval. Having just started my first semester with Ridley College and waiting on news regarding my father's health, I had more than enough to keep me occupied.

43
NO BEARS

With my first semester and exams completed, Jeff and I jumped on a plane heading to the USA. My dad was coming to the end his twelve-week chemo session. It was heartbreaking to see him so frail and helpless.

It's not right to try and gauge where someone's faith is. However, I knew that for most of his life Dad had believed that it was all about ticking all the boxes, doing good and going to church once a week. My father was now on a journey where he was experiencing Jesus on a deeper level. Being extremely conservative and a real traditionalist, it would normally have been well out of my dad's comfort zone to be prayed for. But not now. Twice a day, the four of us – Daddy, Kathleen, Jeff and I – sat and prayed for healing, clarity and wisdom on the way forward. These moments together I will never forget. I felt a connection I had never felt with my dad before.

'We'll see you both in a week,' I gave Daddy and Kathleen a big hug. 'Call if you need us, but you guys could probably do with a rest from visitors.' Daddy was balancing himself on his walker but still managed to wave as we drove away. My heart felt like it was breaking.

So as not to be a burden, Jeff and I had decided to take a short break in the middle of our visit. We were now driving to the Smoky

Mountains National Park and had booked into a chalet where Walt Disney had stayed while filming Davy Crockett.

'How awesome it would be if we saw some bears,' I suggested, as we made our way up the hiking trail.

'Not sure I would know what to do if I saw one,' joked Jeff.

'I thought Australians were capable of tackling most things out in the bush,' I laughed.

'Only one problem: there are no bears in Australia.'

'Crocodile Dundee didn't have a problem with adapting.'

We were on the first day of our four-day walking holiday on the Appalachian Trail, and it was absolutely awesome. Both Jeff and I were mentally and emotionally exhausted, so this gave us time to process our thoughts and feelings. The chalet was idyllic. It was located in a lush forest up in the mountains, not too far from the main hotel, which we strolled to each night for local wine and fresh home-cooked food. This was just what the doctor ordered! But there was another dark cloud looming.

'Jeff wake up, your phone has been beeping for the last couple of hours,' I murmured.

It was 6 a.m. and light had just started streaming through the curtains. I'd been woken up by the constant beeping but had chosen to ignore it. I thought it was probably Jeff's work. But after a while, in my gut I felt something was wrong. Jeff rolled over and unplugged his phone.

'It's my mum saying to call urgently.'

As Jeff listened to his mum, I knew by the expression on his face that it was bad news. I realized from hearing just one side of the conversation that Neil, his stepfather, had just passed away. This was half expected, as he had been a bit like a cat with nine lives. He had experienced strokes and heart attacks over a ten-year period, but each time he'd bounced back. We sat on the bed looking at each other, wondering what to do.

Jeff and I had a dilemma. Should we rush back to Australia? We still had another week planned with Daddy and Kathleen, and we were unsure whether we would see my dad again, as he was fading fast. Jeff made the call.

'Mum, I'm sorry but could we put Neil's funeral on hold for ten days? This will give us time with Iona's father.' I sat listening. In true Australian humour, Jeff finished the call with, 'Great! Put him on ice, with a couple of tinnies (beers). We'll see you in ten days.'

I could hear Judy laughing. Neil liked his beer, wine and spirits, so he would have been okay with this. After a week in Aiken with Daddy and Kathleen and a one-day turnaround in Dubai, we were on our way to Australia.

After saying farewell to Neil, we arrived back in Dubai ready to fight another battle.

44
TIME WARP

'Iona, we'd like you to give your testimony in a couple of weeks at church,' said Fusi.

'Seriously? That would be awesome. Thank you.'

He went on explain that he was wanting to gradually introduce women in to speaking and preaching roles within the church. For a Regions Beyond church, this was stepping into new territory. 'This is the start of something very new, so let's take people on a journey and see what happens.'

A couple of months earlier, Jeff and I had made the decision to move from Gateway Church to its sister church, City Hill. We both felt we could be more actively involved in the City Hill community and Fusi was also very eager to push women's gifting to the forefront. But as we found out, the devil doesn't give up easily.

I gave my testimony and had a lot of great feedback. A month later, I was put on the preaching rota.

***

At about the same time, we left for a two-week holiday to Scotland. We had planned a one-week retreat on the island of Iona, on the west coast of Scotland. My parents had named me after the island, so this was emotionally a very important trip. They had spent a couple of holidays on the island and had agreed that if they had a girl, Iona would be her name. They spoke about the island a great deal and how it had played a major role in the spread of Christianity across Europe.

We stepped off the ferry and onto the Island of Iona. Finally, after 56 years, I was here. I had waited for this moment for a long time. Jeff and I were escorted up to the beautiful stone Abbey where we would be staying along with sixty other guests. We had registered on a residential course on the subject of how Christianity and Islam could work together.

'Blimey you can't even swing a cat in this room!' Jeff was right. We had been warned that the accommodation was basic, but this was a little bit of a shock.

'I'll have the top bunk bed. It doesn't look that stable and I'd prefer not to be crushed to death if the bed collapses,' I insisted laughing.

We put the suitcases hard up against the wall and positioned them on top of each other, then went off to check out the amenities. The other slight concern was that there were only two showers, and I knew there were forty women booked in. This was going to be entertaining!

The first evening we all gathered in the large refectory for dinner.

'Okay, listen up please. We need to put you in your groups for the week,' said a large rosy-faced lady, who looked a bit like a schoolteacher.

Groups of what? I thought.

'You will be in one of these groups: Otters, Puffins or Seals. Listen out for your name.'

I whispered to Jeff, 'This reminds me of school.'

He nodded, winked and smiled, 'This sounds like fun.'

'Each group will be assigned different tasks, from household duties to kitchen chores during the week.'

The next bit of news was that our Christian lecturer was now unable to attend the course, which left a young Muslim professor from Cork University with a group of sixty Christian priests, pastors and missionaries for the week. But this turned out to be a blessing. The Islamic professor was a real character, who knew his stuff and could hold a room without any problem.

Within the daily schedule there were two to three services in the Abbey church.

I was really expecting to have some amazing spiritual experience during our prayer and worship times but, strangely, nothing. Maybe it was because I was struggling with the strict timetable and the dos and don'ts of the daily schedule. This was like a blast from the past, a reminder of my convent school days.

On the first night we decided not to go to the second evening service but instead went in search of a pub. As we strolled down to the ferry port holding hands, I felt sad. I wasn't expecting to feel so overwhelmed and hadn't realized the affect my convent days had had on me.

'I feel miserable and guilty at the same time. We should be with everybody else at the prayer service,' I remarked.

We stepped into the pub and could not believe our eyes. We weren't the only ones who had ventured out. Everyone was there, including the Abbey's volunteers and our professor. It was a time of bonding and making new friends.

Daily walks around the lush green island gave us another opportunity to make new and lasting friends. On one such occasion, as we returned from a hike, to our surprise Jeff's phone rang. This was unexpected, as there was barely a phone signal on the island.

'I can hardly hear you,' shouted Jeff.

He walked off to see if he could get a better signal. Knowing this could take a while, I'd found a little rock to sit on and shut down into daydreaming mode.

'Iona, I'm sorry.' Jeff looked upset. My immediate thought was that it was my dad. Had something happened?

'What?'

'They've taken your name off the preaching rota at church.'

'Why?'

'Some people were not happy with having a woman preaching. Fusi felt that it was perhaps too much too soon and that the church isn't ready for it yet.'

I was very disappointed. Before coming on this holiday, I had spent a lot of time preparing for the sermon. It had taken me three weeks of research, study and prayer. I was due to preach the weekend we arrived back in Dubai.

'I don't know what to say. I know I shouldn't take it personally, but it's difficult not to.'

***

When we embarked on the second part of our holiday, which was going to be a walking holiday, we both opted to veg out at the hotel and read instead. I was unable to pray or read the Bible. I felt like I had fallen into a dark hole of disappointment and was clutching at the sides trying to pull myself up. What had happened? Where was God? For the first time in years, I went out and bought a fictional book. I never read fiction. I love biographies and non-fiction books, and of course the bestseller, the Bible. But I could not bring myself to read anything that related to fact or truth.

I immersed myself in my detective thriller while sitting in front of the fire in the hotel lounge. The hotel was situated on a beautiful loch, surrounded by the most stunning countryside. We went out on small walks, sat around the fire, ate good food and drank great wine. But the best thing was having an en suite bathroom. After a week of getting up at 4.30 in the morning to beat the long queue for a two-minute shower, this was heaven on earth.

Our vacation finished in Glasgow, where we had a couple of days before flying back to Dubai. Jeff had left one day earlier, as he needed to go via London, so it gave me time to gather my thoughts.

I prayed for guidance and opened my Bible. God spoke to me almost immediately. He led me to 2 Corinthians 4:16–18 (NIV) which says, 'Therefore we do not lose heart. Though outwardly we are wasting away, yet inwardly we are being renewed day by day. For our light and momentary troubles are achieving for us an eternal glory that far outweighs them all. So we fix our eyes not on what is seen, but on what is unseen, since what is seen is temporary, but what is unseen is eternal.' These words resonated deep within me. I felt like I was beginning to climb back out of my hole and refocus on what was important. I have no idea what happened to me on the island of Iona but I know that one day I need to go back and maybe I will get some answers? For now, we had more pressing family issues.

45
GOODBYE SWEETHEART

One month prior to our trip to Iona, we had been given the news that Jeff's mum, Judy, had been diagnosed with pancreatic cancer. So, we were not surprised when the call came.

'Jeff, it's your sister Pam,' I handed Jeff my mobile.

'Okay, we'll have a look at flights and let you know.' He looked so sad as he told me, 'The doctor is recommending that we fly now.'

We had literally just returned from our holiday and we were back in the air. It just seemed like an endless flow of bad news. We were still coming to terms with losing Jeff's stepfather Neil 12 months earlier.

Judy was a real fighter and was not one for lying around, but she had become so frail that it was now up to the family to step in. Pam, Jeff's half-sister is a carer, as is one of her daughters, so they took it in turn to stay over as Judy didn't want to leave her home. We spent many hours giggling and sharing fond memories. But there was one incident that I would never forget.

As Judy was too weak to get to church, we had arranged for her close friends to join us in a worship and communion service at the farm. There were nine of us in her living room. Judy lay on the couch and we all huddled together. When Lyndon the vicar (who had now replaced Bruce) started praying, the whole atmosphere in the room changed. It was as if Jesus had walked in. I was so emotionally overwhelmed that I could not speak, and I struggled to hold back the tears. Looking around the room it was obvious that I wasn't the only one feeling these emotions.

'What just happened there was unbelievable,' remarked Judy.

'I think Jesus arrived in the room,' I agreed.

'Well, we need to do that again next Monday.' Judy was overwhelmed, as we all were.

Six days later, Judy passed on.

Her funeral was one of pure celebration. She knew that she was stepping into a new life and wanted all those attending to experience the same joy and hope that she had. Jeff gave the eulogy, which was funny and emotional; I gave the message, which is not easy when you're mourning a loved one, but it's what Judy wanted. I preached her favourite sermon, which included a prop: a very long piece of rope with a bit of red adhesive tape at the end. The rope illustrated our time in eternity which goes on for ever and ever, while the tiny red bit of tape on the very end represented our time on planet earth. Francis Chan, an American pastor, came up with this very clever way of demonstrating that what we put our trust in on earth determines where we will be for eternity.

The funeral directors were slightly bemused by the service, which ended with a big photo of Judy smiling and waving with a Christmas hat on, followed by one of her favourite songs 'Goodnight Sweetheart' as her coffin was carried out.

All went smoothly that day except for a bee attack!

I had stayed on to help clean up the church, while Jeff and over a hundred guests headed back to our farm for the wake. When I eventually arrived home, I knew immediately something had happened. There were kids crying and adults looking extremely distressed.

'What happened Jeff?' I asked.

'I have never seen anything like it. A mammoth swarm of bees appeared, stretching a hundred metres in length, blocking people from getting to the house.'

'Wow that's weird!'

Most of the guests ran through the swarm, as did the children, and many got stung. Strangely, the bees never came near the house, they just blocked people from coming onto our veranda and then they just disappeared. Thankfully, no one was seriously hurt, and with good food and drinks flowing, it was soon forgotten about.

Losing both of Jeff's parents within a year and with my father terminally ill, Jeff and I were emotionally drained and slightly battered. But I had come to realize how precious time with our loved ones is – something we should never take for granted.

**

We returned to Dubai and everything went back to the normal routine fairly quickly. But within a month, I had the urge for a change. I was on my way to the dentist when I took a wrong turn and ended up driving past our old villa. Draped over the wall was a 'For Rent' sign. I then noticed our favourite coffee house situated at the end of the road and, out of the blue, I had this feeling that it was time to move back to the city. By the time I arrived at the dentist, a plan was already beginning to formulate in my mind.

I messaged Jeff, 'I think we should move back into Dubai.' I was confident that God had laid seeds in my heart – it felt right. And the thought came from out of the blue – that's a God move. Until that morning, Jeff and I had been more than happy living out at Desert Palms. We had moved back there two years earlier. It was our second time living there, but this time without the horses. We loved being surrounded by polo fields, horses and desert wildlife.

Jeff agreed that it was time to move. We asked the Lord to lead us to the right house in the right location, and he did just that. Within a week we had found a villa that ticked all the boxes. Six weeks later, we were in. It was a modern villa with glass windows that stretched from floor to ceiling and an open-plan lower floor with an indoor–outdoor pool. Jeff wasn't keen on having a pool, probably because he must be the only Australian alive who cannot swim. Our new home was ideally located for us to open up our house and be more active in the community.

Divine confirmation on our relocation came shortly after moving in.

'Wake up Jeff, wake up,' I was nudging Jeff's arm.

He groaned and muttered, 'You're kidding me. It's the middle of the night.'

'I had this dream; it was so real. I touched an angel.'

'Iona, please, can we discuss this in the morning.' Jeff rolled over and went back to sleep, and I lay awake stunned. Did I really just experience that?

In my dream, I was standing in our new living room speaking to several people who were standing in front of the large glass windows that reached way up to the roofline. As I was talking, I saw a huddle of angels descending and ascending behind the glass. I was so mesmerized by them that I slowly walked towards them, and then the glass seemed to disappear. The angels just kept going up and down but then one of the angels brushed my arm and I was suddenly overwhelmed by an emotion I've never felt before and would struggle to describe. It was like peace, joy and bliss all rolled into one; it was so powerful that I felt myself pass out.

The next morning, while walking the dogs and having breakfast, I kept rambling on and on to Jeff in detail about everything that had happened. He remained silent: no comments, no wise remarks, he just decided to remain in mute mode.

I recorded my experience in my journal and also drew what I had seen. I then went on a research mission to find out more about angels. It was fascinating but also sad to learn how we have almost dismissed angels from our churches. Billy Graham, one of the greatest evangelists that ever lived, states in his book *God's Secret Agents*: 'Angels are God's messengers whose chief business is to carry out his orders in the world.'

Even with all my research, at one point I was beginning to wonder if the angels were all in my head, but confirmation came that my encounter was very real. As part of the City Hill Church, we had organized a Wednesday Prayer, Praise and Pizza (PPP) evening at our new house. Our first gathering was a month after we had moved in.

There were ten of us praying in our living room, when Joe suddenly said, 'I see this house surrounded by angels and they are descending and ascending.' Jeff nearly fell over backwards. He looked over at me with a 'That's amazing!' expression. My heart leapt, *Thank you Lord*. I went on to tell everyone in the room about my dream. I showed them my journal and the pictures I'd drawn. It was as though God wanted to reaffirm that the angels were here in this place. That evening, the Holy Spirit touched each of us in an extraordinary way. On a humorous note, Joe wanted to speak to Jeff and me privately after everyone had gone home. He said he had not mentioned everything he saw because he was a little embarrassed.

'I also saw angels surrounding your dogs. They are there to care for and protect them.'

I smiled and said, 'What about the cats?' Again, this was another confirmation of something we couldn't make sense of. Since arriving at the villa, Louie, one of our rescued Chinese Crested dogs, had been cured of his bowl disease. He had previously been given six months to live. Louie was now off medication and leaping around like a spring lamb.

Our bi-weekly PPP group grew and became central to our community life in Dubai. Even though it started as a City Hill Church gathering, we now had people from other denominations joining us. We were now up to twenty people from nine nations, from doctors to insurance brokers, the unemployed to schoolteachers. We were a real mixed, quirky bunch who had one thing in common – we lived and breathed Jesus. The move from the desert to the city had come with many blessings. The other blessing was that Fusi had finally won his battle to allow women in preaching roles. Things seemed to be travelling in the right direction, and so were Jeff and I!

46
FINISHING LAST

I whispered to Jeff, 'This is what you call a community church. One that gets out there and helps those in need.' He nodded.

We were at Bay City Church in Cape Town, South Africa, standing next to Sheldon and Kathleen Kidwell, the minister and his wife. I had met them in India at the Regions Beyond Leadership Conference and knew immediately we were kindred spirits. This was our first visit to the Cape and we had fallen in love with the city and this church community. We clapped and jumped up and down in delight as we watched one of the gang leaders in the area get baptised.

Bay City's philosophy was one of getting out into the city and putting into action what they believed – to help those in need. Everything was community driven. The next day we were able to experience one of the projects they had started.

'This is the first time I've seen anything like this,' I said to Anton who ran the Sozo Foundation.

Jeff agreed. 'What you're doing here is incredible.'

Sozo was originally created out of Bay City and now is run as a non-profit organization in the middle of a very poor area. The centre provides training for the local youth, giving them the skill sets to step into jobs – from baristas, to bakers, carpenters and graphic design training – so they can support themselves and their families. The

Sozo Foundation was for Jeff and me inspirational. So much so that by the time I got back to Dubai, I was wanting to get out of my box and do more. It was a great feeling to be part of a community and be able to preach, but I needed to get out of my comfort zone.

For the next few months I went on a quest to find my next calling. Bay City community had inspired me and had given me a new perspective. In my enthusiasm, I jumped in with all four feet without asking God for guidance. I restarted looking at the possibility of going through the process of ordination to become a priest with the Anglican Church in Dubai. Even though I had provisionally been accepted in Australia, we'd had to stop the process because I was now spending more time in the Middle East. Unfortunately, after a couple of months I realized that God was closing the door on ordination in Dubai. I knew this was not the right time or place. My theology degree had also ground to a halt because of my travel routine. I felt like a dog chasing its tail. I was going round and round in circles. I was going nowhere!

Then God stepped in and said 'Stop!' I know I can be a bit inclined to dash off in one direction, and when I hit a brick wall, I know it's because I was going off on my own rather than waiting to find out what God wanted me to do. This is where I was now, bruised and lying next to another brick wall.

I sat in our living room, surrounded by our pets. We were now up to five cats and four dogs, all of which had been rescued except Lady Bella – our zoo and our family! Jeff was away in Iraq working on a new project. I had no projects except one, which was to finish the large canvas painting of my angel dream. *What now Lord? What do I do?*

Then I remembered one of the dreams he had given me. It was when everyone else seemed to be in full flight, out there doing stuff for God's kingdom, while I was sitting around doing nothing, similar to how I felt right now.

I had dreamt that I was in a race, a running race, and that every other competitor was overtaking me. I was becoming more and more stressed as people flew past me, while my legs were getting heavier and heavier. I could see the finish line but was frustrated because I was behind everybody. When I crossed the line, in what seemed like last place, a little man came running up to me jumping up and down with such joy shouting, 'You won! You won!' and proceeded to hang a medal around my neck. I tried to explain to him that he must have been looking at the wrong race because I had come in last. But he kept saying, 'You won! You won!' Then suddenly, I woke up.

That morning at breakfast I was praying for clarification when it dawned on me that God was showing me that we are all in a race, but if we keep our eyes focused just on him then yes, we will win. It doesn't matter what others are doing, we must not compare ourselves with them, as we are all on a different path. If we focus on other humans, it detracts from what God has planned for us. Plus, sometimes he puts us in a lay-by while he shapes and moulds us for the next part of the journey. God cannot work with us if we are preoccupied with what others are doing. By depending solely on him, a path will open up that is uniquely for us. If we go our own way, our gifting cannot be utilized. It's all about running our own race, not someone else's. The Bible tells us in Ephesians 2:10 (NIV), 'For we are God's handiwork, created in Christ Jesus to do good works, which God prepared in advance for us to do.' He has already planned our race, and the only way to stay on track is by not letting go of God's hand.

As I sat on the sofa surrounded by my furry friends, I realised that now was a time to be in that lay-by, to sit and wait, to stop racing for the moment. My thoughts turned to the last forty years and how patient God had been. Every time I turned away, he had come after me. He had every intention of rescuing me. That's a love I cannot even describe!

I looked at our menagerie of dogs and cats sprawled on sofas, chairs and my lap and wondered what would have happened to them if we hadn't rescued them. Likewise with many of our horses: I liked the rejects, the broken, the rebels and the untameable ones. I chuckled to myself. I had worked hard over the years to tame horses, dogs and cats, most of which were broken and rejected. In a way, God had been doing the same with me. I was broken, and am still partially broken. But every day another piece of me gets put back into its rightful place.

I am still very competitive, but now I'm competitive for God. Many people say that competitiveness is ungodly. Having a strong desire to achieve and succeed is not wrong, as long as we put God first. When I surrendered the controls (reins) of my life to the one who created me then, and only then, did I live the life that God intended – one that has given me freedom and a purpose. Yes, I keep getting it wrong. I'm human with many flaws but, thankfully, God is always there to put me back together and place me into the correct race – one that I'm determined to win, even if I do come last!

EPILOGUE (SNIPPETS)

Just as I was coming to the end of my first draft of this book, my father passed away: 3 December 2018. His funeral was a celebration of his life. He had lived a full life, but it was only in the last couple of years that he experienced a real sense of what life is all about and that what was before him was just the beginning of something greater.

***

God's timing!

I woke up one morning and sensed that God wanted us to go back and visit our first Dubai church, Gateway, specifically in two weeks' time. We had left two years previously, though we had stayed in contact with Pete and Liz. Jeff wasn't convinced that this was a good move, and half way to the church I also doubted my decision and told Jeff to pull over and turn around. But he carried on driving!

When we got to Gateway, Pete the minister was so happy to see us, but he also looked very shocked.

'Why did you come today?' he asked.

'You'll have to ask God that one,' I said. 'I have no idea.'

It was a joy to be reunited with our friends. The worship was awesome, and God's presence was overpowering. The whole atmosphere felt different, it was electric. Then came a real shock. Pete stood up and announced that women would now be preaching in Gateway. Jeff turned to me and grinned. God had bought us there on that morning specifically to hear this.

***

As this book was coming to its final stages, me and my Australian friend Kate went to a three-day Christian conference 'Awakening Australia' in Melbourne. On the last-but-one day, Bill Johnson, one of the speakers from the USA, asked anyone who had ear problems to stand, as he wanted to pray for healing. I am not shy in coming forward, so I was one of the first to leap to my feet. One week later, I realized that my benign positional vertigo (BPV) had completely gone. Totally healed! After seven years of not being able to lie down flat and always having to sleep with three pillows, this was incredible. Having BPV had stopped me from doing any form of exercise like Pilates or gym work, as I kept losing my balance. So yes, God heals, in a mighty way.

For the first time in years, I'm back in the gym. Will I rush off and start competing? Good question! My personal trainer Milan would love me to start bodybuilding, but I think that God may have other plans!

***

So, what now?

From my early years as a sportsperson I had been passionate about living in the present moment and experiencing an awareness that allowed me to focus on the now. We miss so much when our minds keep drifting out of the present moment. But more importantly, we can miss God's quiet voice. You cannot communicate with God without a connection, and that happens only when we focus on him and him alone. So many get frustrated because they cannot hear or know God's will for their lives. We need to stop and listen and be aware, be mindful. We are great at speaking and asking for stuff, but we need to stop and listen to what God wants to say. This is where I am right now. In a lay-by listening and spending time in God's presence. Not asking for anything, just resting at his feet. The Bible tells us specifically not to focus on the past or the future but to live out today in God's presence. Because I am competitive, I find being still and not 'doing' difficult. But the rewards of spending time with him are beyond anything imaginable.

If you have been blessed or challenged by this book, please write and tell me about it.
Many Blessings

Iona Rossely
iona.rossely@gmail.com
www.ionarossely.com